K2

DREAMS AND REALITY

JIM HABERL

ACKNOWLEDGEMENTS

Anyone who has climbed on the world's great mountains or written a book knows that success with either project would be impossible without the help and encouragement of friends. Because this book is really a mixture of the two, the list of people I would like to recognize is so long it would require too many pages; I have valued your support over the years.

As for K2, I would like to thank my teammates: Phil, Stacy, John, Steve, Dan, John, Yousaf, Ghulam and Muhammad Ali. Others were a part of our journey in many ways, I credit them as well.

This book took a much different kind of effort. I am grateful to the following people who took the time to share ideas, read the text and pass judgement or simply reassure me in my work: Pat Haberl, Kevin Haberl, Susan Pendakur, Alan Greer, Larry Emrick, Phil Powers, John Petroske, Glenda Bennion, Eric Boyum, Chris Harris, Ian McSorley, Kelly Brooks, Brad Nickason, Tom Ellison, David Freeze, Michael Down, Matthew MacEachern, Pat Morrow, Bernie Lyon, Stephan Fuller and Brian Scrivener. Bob Herger told me it would work and then showed me how. Many thanks to publisher Vic Marks and the staff at the Typeworks who shared their knowledge and experience. Susan Oakey stood by me as I went to the mountain, then again as I went through the process of creating this book. I am especially thankful for her loving patience and understanding. And through the years my parents, Bill and Margaret Haberl, have supported my lifestyle and stood behind me in every way. Their love could never be returned.

All photography by Jim Haberl except the following: page 28, 34, 52 by Dan Culver; page 38 by Troy Kirwan; page 67 by Phil Powers; page 83, 86 by John Haigh.

Studio Photography by Bob Herger.
Illustrations by Bernie Lyon - Studio B Graphics, Vancouver, BC
Edited by Brian Scrivener

Designed by Vic Marks and Stephen Gregory
Typeset by The Typeworks, Vancouver, B.C.
Printed and bound in China

Canadian Cataloguing in Publication Data
Haberl, Jim, 1958–
K2, Dreams and Reality

(Raincoast Journeys)
ISBN 1-55192-267-3

1. Haberl, Jim, 1958- –Journeys–Pakistan.
2. Mountaineering–Pakistan–K2 (Mountain)
3. K2 (Pakistan: Mountain)–Description and travel. I. Title II. Title: K two III. Series
GV199.44.P182K1825 1999   796.5'22'095491
C98-911177-6

To order copies of this book:
Contact Raincoast Books, 8680 Cambie St.
Vancouver, B.C. V6P 6M9
(604) 323-7100

HALF-TITLE
The South face of K2
from Concordia

TITLE PAGE
Full moon rising
over Mitre Peak

To Dan:

A friend who sensed what life was and lived it.

PHIL, DAN AND I climbed slowly together and stopped as we reached the crest of the ridge at 8000 metres. I collapsed heavily in the snow, as if someone had kicked me behind the knees. I was thankful for the rest — my mind and body barely able to stay ahead of our task. Between deep breaths, I fought with the knot in the rope and the locking carabiner on my harness, a procedure that would have been routine back home in the Coast Mountains of British Columbia. But mitts and knots never seem to mix, especially here, half a world away.

I looked up and saw Phil methodically putting on his high altitude suit. Smart, I thought. When the sun dropped below the bulk of the mountain above, the temperature would cool off dramatically, plunging well below freezing. I was already wearing my suit, though I had little on underneath. The day had been warmer than we could have imagined at this altitude, rising to 10 or more degrees celsius, and I had stripped off most of my inner layers of clothing. To put them back on here would mean taking off my harness and boots. That job would have to wait until I was inside a tent. Phil had chosen to climb in his layers and was now putting on his bright red, goose-down suit over the top of everything. I envied his situation but decided not to try to fix mine. I stopped thinking about clothing.

Dan untied from the rope and was continuing toward the uppermost bivouac on our route, Camp 4, still a gruelling day's climb below the summit. I sat in the snow and thought about how tough it was just to function at these heights; the climbing was as physically and mentally demanding as anything I had ever done. Meanwhile, my mitted fingers persevered with the knot.

Camp was only two hundred metres away. Combatting my lethargy, I stood up and coiled the rope. As a precaution against the possibility of a fall into a

Dan Culver climbs the final few steps to Camp 4 at 8050 metre on K2's Abruzzi Ridge.

crevasse, we had roped up that morning when we had left Camp 3. But that hazard was now behind us and Dan was slowly ascending the broad ridge above. The snow had been windswept and compressed by the storms that scour the mountain almost every day of the year, so there was no foot penetration, only crampon marks in the hard snow. On a lower peak the climbing would be easy. Near the top of this giant, every move was an effort – five deep breaths, an attempt to satisfy my body's demand for oxygen, before the next step could be taken towards our goal. Phil and I exchanged tired glances and I fell quietly in line behind Dan, his lonely imprints in the snow urging me upward.

Camp 4 was a bleak and windswept place, completely exposed to the awesome power of nature at that height. The savage intensity of the storms that ravage the upper slopes of the mountain can only be imagined because it would be unlikely that a person could live through one. The only hint that anyone had ever been in that barren place was the abandoned remains of a tent from the Slovenian attempt on the summit just a few weeks earlier.

When I finally arrived at Camp 4, 8050 metres, I dropped my pack and vomited. There was no food in my stomach. The high altitude had prevented me from eating anything for two days and all that came up was the foul, green bile of an empty belly. Immediately I began to shiver from the cold. I needed to get out of the wind. Phil had our tent in his pack and he was still several minutes below. The only shelter was the Slovenian tent. Wind-drifted snow was creeping up its walls and the nylon fabric was taut with pressure. Dan grappled with the door zipper, fighting to clear it of ice and snow. He won and gratefully I crawled inside.

I felt weak and very small in such a high and wild place.

While I wrestled with putting on additional layers of clothing under my altitude suit, I could hear Dan and Phil outside setting up our tent and preparing for the night. Phil passed the radio inside and I made the 5:00 PM call to our Base Camp, three kilometres below us. Our luck was holding out; the weather forecast, from our friends the Swedes, sounded perfect for an attempt on the summit the following day. The Swedish team in Base Camp had a radio link with their national meteorological service in Stockholm which was transmitting satellite weather forecasts for the area. Their latest facsimile message, combined with a steady barometer and light winds from the north, provided us with great news.

Once our little tent was up, Phil escaped the cold in it while Dan came into the Slovenian tent with me and lit the lightweight butane stove. Soon the small gas burner was humming, warming our tent and melting snow for drinks.

Dan did most of the cooking that night, a tedious chore at high altitude. For three hours we carefully melted chunks of dry snow in our small pot, making cup after cup of warm fluid to replace the liquid our bodies had lost from the day of climbing. Phil and Dan drank their mugs of soup, hot chocolate and tea while I sipped with difficulty at my cup of warm water. The thought of any taste, even tea, made me nauseous, so I quietly leaned back against the wall of the tent and forced myself to drink the water.

Eventually Dan left me and joined Phil in the small, two-person tent we had carried to Camp 4. Phil slept in his thick, down suit and two lightweight overbags — a system he had chosen on the ascent from Camp 3 in order to lighten his pack. Dan and I, still wearing our insulated suits, curled up in our much warmer, four-season sleeping bags. It was 8:00 PM and the alarm was set for midnight.

If the weather was right and the effect of altitude on our bodies overnight was not too severe, the next day would bring our summit bid. I lay quietly in my bag and listened to myself. My mind measured the deep fatigue of my body as it laboured to contend with the difficult breathing and fits of coughing. It seemed the altitude had completely drained my physical reserves.

I knew I would never be closer to the top.

I wanted to climb the mountain.

I asked myself what role ambition was playing in my decision-making. Before leaving North America I had promised myself that ambition would only influence me in a small way on this mountain, but its impact, after so much effort and cost, can become dangerous. I was physically very weak and wondered if I was simply too slow to adapt to these great heights. From their outward appearance, Phil and Dan seemed to be doing much better than I.

Yet I wanted to climb the mountain.

I dozed uneasily. At 10:30 PM I woke up gasping for air and gripped with terror. Where was I? Anxious and alone, I stared into the blackness of the tent. I tried to relax and boost my confidence with thoughts of all the other climbing expeditions I had endured to cold and desolate places. Experience. I sipped some water and slipped back into a deeper rest.

Phil and Dan also slept fitfully. The alarm rang at midnight. I could not muster any energy and again it was Dan who fired the stove and filled the pot with snow for drinks. Dan and I retreated into our goose down cocoons, while Phil searched longingly for the warm spot in his lightweight setup. We were all half awake and hiding from the reality of our tired bodies and the icy temperatures outside.

More than two hours later the stove was turned off and we inched our way out of the tents. The moon was bright and full and only a slight breeze swept down from above. The summit of K2, the second highest peak in the world and the mountain of our dreams, was beckoning us with the rare privilege to try for the top.

OVERLEAF →

Sunrise on the upper slopes of K2 from Concordia.

K 2 — D R E A M S A N D R E A L I T Y

CHINA

K2

PAKISTAN

NEPAL

EVEREST ▲

INDIA

INDIAN
OCEAN

The Himalayas

K2 IS LOCATED ON THE Pakistan-China border in the Karakoram Mountains, a vast chain of spectacular summits. Though technically a trans-Himalayan range, separated from the main Himalayan crest by the Indus River, from a mountaineer's perspective the Karakoram peaks are effectively a part of the world's greatest range – the Himalayas. At 8611 metres above sea level, K2 dominates its surroundings like a monarch on a throne. The only peak on the planet which reaches higher into the sky is Mount Everest, over 1200 kilometres south and east of K2 on the border of China and the renowned mountain kingdom of Nepal, and only 237 metres higher than the peak we had come to climb.

The heights of the Karakoram offer everything that a mountaineer could ask for or dream of. No range can surpass the scope of the challenges on the peaks of Northern Pakistan. Towering granite walls, with their sculptured beauty and blank faces, dare climbers to test their technique and persistence. Sheer ridges of rock and ice rise for thousands of metres to fabled summits providing some of the world's most difficult technical mountain routes. And the Karakoram contains the great test of altitude. There are only fourteen summits in the world which rise above the lofty height of 8000 metres; four of those elusive peaks are centred in the heart of the Karakoram. K2 is the second highest mountain on Earth and arguably the most difficult to climb.

The names of the peaks alone are an inspiration to the imagination of mountaineers. Mountain lore is full of tales on summits like Trango, The Ogre, K2, Gasherbrum, Latok, Nameless Tower, Hidden Peak, Paiju, Masherbrum – each mountain has adventure and human drama associated with it. Often tragedy.

Mountaineers build their dreams on images of the Karakoram. A single photograph. A moment in time. The warm glow of sunrise on a summit ridge. The dramatic play of storm clouds across a steep face. A climber striving for a distant summit. Only a brief impression, but enough to entice people to dream. The spark which sets a fire in a climber's heart. The yearning for adventure, to explore and climb in high places. Spectacular and inspiring, the Karakoram is a magical place where climbers can realize their dreams.

RIGHT

Sunset on Masherbrum, one of the giants of the Karakoram. The 7821 metre peak was first climbed in 1960 by Americans George Bell and Willi Unsoeld.

→ OVERLEAF

A spectacular view of the Karakoram from Camp 2 on K2's Abruzzi Ridge. The Godwin-Austen Glacier flows to Concordia in the left of the picture while Masherbrum rises above the lower summits.

In the summer of 1991 Stacy Allison of Portland, Oregon – the first American woman to climb Mount Everest – applied to the government of Pakistan for permission to make an attempt on K2. Three months later she received her response. It was positive. With that approval in hand, Stacy began the process of organizing a K2 expedition.

Aspiring to such a task with any hope of success requires preparation, money, enthusiasm, luck, climbing skill, experience and teamwork. Though every element of such an expedition is important, by far the most critical ingredient is the team. The compatibility of the members and the common desire to achieve the goal is essential. Ultimately, the unit will share untold demands and emotions: satisfaction and hardship, joy and frustration, possible success – but more likely failure to reach the elusive and dangerous summit of K2. All of these challenges take place over a period of two or three months, often in close quarters under difficult conditions. Stacy did an excellent job of assembling such a team – the 1993 American and Canadian K2 Expedition.

The 1993 American and Canadian K2 Expedition at Camp 1 – 6000 metres. From the left: Jim Haberl, Stacy Allison, Phil Powers, John Haigh, Steve Steckmyer, Dan Culver (kneeling), John Petroske.

ARLY IN THE MORNING of May 23, 1993 we landed in Rawalpindi, Pakistan. It was 2:00 AM and still very dark outside. Looking out the tiny window from my seat in the airplane, it was hard to get any sense of the unknown country we were entering. Tired but excited, the seven of us shuffled down the crowded aisle of the Pakistan International Airlines Boeing 747. As we stepped off the plane, our senses were immediately assaulted by the heat rising off the tarmac. The night-time air temperature was a stifling 32 degrees celsius. We had arrived.

Our team had left North America loaded down with 1500 kilograms of gear — forty-six boxes and bags. Every piece weighed at least the maximum thirty-three kilograms allowed by the airline and each was stuffed with food, equipment, rope and clothing — testing the limits of what seams and zippers could manage. Luckily, we lost nothing in the airplane transfers at New York or Frankfurt. When it all rolled off the luggage ramp we were left surrounded by our mountain of possessions and a sea of brown-uniformed porters scrambling and shouting for our business. Exhausted by the crossing of time zones and too many hours in the cramped, smoke-filled plane, none of us were too eager to deal with the chaos.

Stacy and Phil took charge and set out in search of our agent, Nazir Sabir, who was scheduled to meet us at the airport. Before long they found Nazir's man, Saed. He introduced himself to us and as we each in turn questioned him about his name, his affable response through a broad, white smile was "Just call me John." For reasons unknown, we breezed through customs without a single bag or box being opened. After that John dealt with the porters and directed us to a private bus waiting outside the terminal.

We drove in darkness for forty minutes to our hotel, The Lodgings Guest House, where air-conditioned rooms and showers with clean towels awaited. Before we could enjoy those amenities, however, we sweated in the sticky night air moving our vast amount of luggage off the bus and into the hotel's courtyard. It was 3:00 AM. John bid us good night and said that he would return first thing in the morning. We slumped into our respective rooms for quick showers and a cool sleep. The freshly laundered sheets smelled wonderful. Two years of preparation were paying off.

Rawalpindi and Islamabad are sister cities. 'Pindi is the old town, a crowded city of narrow, winding bazaars and ancient buildings crammed together into a chaotic and colourful mix. By contrast, Islamabad is modern, spacious and new. The building of the new city, which began in 1961, continues today with emphasis on wide avenues lined with shady trees and contemporary buildings. It is a conscious creation of a new capital for Pakistan replacing the humid, coastal city of Karachi.

Our days in Islamabad were hot and scarcely bearable — the afternoon temperatures reaching 46 degrees celsius. Fiery air rose off the black city streets in waves, searing our nostrils. But worse, the oppressive heat made the mandatory bureau-cratic responsibilities more tedious than usual. We were in Pakistan to climb K2, but to get there we had first to scale a mountain of paper. What saved our sanity in the city was Stacy's foresight and organized manner, the air conditioning in our hotel and the ice cream parlour down the street!

In Islamabad we were joined by two very different people who would both be-come important team members as well as friends. Captain Mir Yousaf Khan was our government-assigned Liaison Officer (LO). An LO accompanies every expedition to a major peak in the Karakoram, acting as an emissary and as a consultant on routes and local customs. There are countless expedition horror stories of LOs who make things more difficult with unreasonable demands and lack of cooperation. With Yousaf it became immediately apparent that he wanted to work with us and be an integral part of our team. We also met our cook, Ghulam Mohammad. Ghulam was a true gentleman and a great resource. Ours would be his ninth trip as a cook to K2 Base Camp. We would come to enjoy his ability to prepare tasty food ranging from tantalizing curry dishes to warm doughnuts, expertly made in a remote mountain setting. Every day at K2, Ghulam would squat on his haunches in his crude, rock-walled kitchen and happily cook creative meals for our team. His experience was in-valuable and he opened his heart to us. We welcomed these two new friends to share our adventure.

Everyone on the team had separate responsibilities while in Islamabad. Stacy

**Our Liaison Officer, Captain
Mir Yousaf Khan.**

assigned daily chores ranging from exchanging each of our American dollars into twenty-eight Pakistani rupees to organizing how our mail was going to get to and from our Base Camp at K2. The initial transaction with our money was done in a carpet shop in Islamabad. The team casually perused carpets and other expensive trinkets until we were led clandestinely upstairs to exchange our money on the black market. The next step was to take taxis to more than ten banks around Islamabad, cleaning out several branches of their small bills as we changed our stack of 500 rupee notes into ones, fives and tens to pay our porters and to buy supplies in Skardu. In the end we had twenty-five kilograms of local paper currency. The postal arrangements were a complex series of stages relying on Nazir Sabir in Islamabad, his contact man in the northern town of Skardu and any trekker or porter who might be walking by K2 and be willing to carry mail in or out of the mountains.

The team's biggest job in town was the huge task of assembling seventy porter loads – each to weigh exactly twenty-five kilograms – from our mound of supplies brought from North America and the new items in the pile, recently bought in the markets in Rawalpindi. That chore was accomplished in searing daytime heat on the driveway behind our hotel.

Our duties took three days to finish. During that time we also had a chance to slow down and share some hours together, laughing and telling stories over fine meals and the odd ice cream sundae. It was an important time, particularly in the early morning and late evening when few K2 responsibilities distracted us. We began the enjoyable, social process of building our team. We would rely on each other for the next three months on a journey to a mountain that would challenge us all, both as individuals and collectively. Those early days in Islamabad provided us with trials of patience and persistence which would establish a foundation for our team that would serve us well in our ultimate test – K2.

Our cook, Ghulam Mohammad.

Metric conversion chart

HEIGHTS:

K2:	8611 metres
	28,244 feet
Everest:	8848 metres
	29,028 feet
Camp 4:	8050 metres
	26,400 feet
Camp 3:	7450 metres
	24,440 feet
Camp 2:	6700 metres
	21,980 feet
Camp 1:	6000 metres
	19,680 feet
ABC:	5250 metres
	17,220 feet
Base Camp:	5000 metres
	16,400 feet

WEIGHTS:

15 kilograms → 33 pounds
25 kilograms → 55 pounds
500 kilograms → 1,100 pounds
1500 kilograms → 3,300 pounds
1700 kilograms → 3,740 pounds
2500 kilograms → 5,500 pounds

DISTANCES:

80 kilometres → 48 miles
1200 kilometres → 720 miles

TEAM MEMBERS

Stacy Allison, a strong mountaineer and competent leader, lives in Portland, Oregon. Stacy was the first American woman to reach the summit of Mount Everest. In addition to her success on the world's highest peak, Stacy's years of climbing have seen ascents of Ama Dablam in Nepal, Pik Communism in the Pamirs, Denali in Alaska and several high summits in South America. Stacy has recently written a book about her climbing accomplishments titled, *Beyond the Limits*.

John Petroske, a computer programmer from Seattle, learned to love the mountains as a young man in Washington's Cascade Range and later on trips to Alaska and Asia. John climbed with Stacy on Mount Everest in 1988 and proved himself a tireless worker and complete team-player. He gave up his chance at reaching the summit of Everest to rescue a Spanish climber on the South Col at 8000 metres. For that act of sacrifice and courage, John was presented the American Alpine Club's Sowles Award for mountaineering heroism. In John, Stacy knew that she had a teammate she could count on.

Phil Powers, the chief mountaineering instructor for the National Outdoor Leadership School in Lander, Wyoming, was recommended to Stacy through mutual friends. Phil had climbed to nearly 8000 metres on K2 in 1993 before being turned back by poor weather. Our trip to K2 would be Phil's fifth expedition into the Karakoram Mountains. On two expeditions in the summer of 1987 he successfully climbed Gasherbrum II and a new route on Latipilla Brak. His big-mountain experience proved invaluable.

John Haigh, an intensive care unit physician practicing in Calgary, Alberta, was on the 1986 Peace Climb Expedition. His home range, the Canadian Rockies, provided a rich training ground for his journeys to big mountains in other parts of Asia. He climbed in the fall of 1994 with John Petroske and Steve Steckmyer on Manaslu, the world's eighth highest mountain. John's medical expertise and mountaineering background made him an integral member of the team.

Steve Steckmyer, a mechanical engineer living in Seattle, Washington, had extensive experience climbing in the Cascades, Canada and Alaska. As well as his attempt on Manaslu with John Haigh and John Petroske, Steve had also climbed in the Indian Himalaya on Shardaren Parbat. His relaxed manner and team orientation made Steve a great member of our K2 expedition.

Dan Culver, an outdoor adventure guide from Vancouver, British Columbia, was the fifth Canadian to climb Mount Everest—an ascent which characterized Dan's passionate determination to achieve with everything in his life. His Everest summit came only four years after he began mountaineering in 1987. Dan's other climbing career included ascents on Canada's Mount Logan, Mount Vinson in Antarctica, Aconcagua in Argentina, two attempts on Thamserku's elegant West Ridge in Nepal and numerous routes in the Coast Mountains of B.C.

B Y MAY 26 WE were ready to leave Islamabad on the next step of our journey to Skardu, a mountain town in northern Pakistan. We held in our hands the paper airline tickets issued in Seattle, but our names could not be found in the electronic memory of the computer in Rawalpindi. Our reservations for the flight from 'Pindi to Skardu got lost somewhere in the computer network between North America and Pakistan. The next available booking for a group our size was August 17. Steve and I pleaded with the man in charge. We sat in his office and shared tea. We even suggested a deal might be worked out. Not a bribe, certainly, but maybe a little something in appreciation for his cooperation. However, try as we did, there was no way of getting our team aboard that flight.

There is only one daily flight to the Skardu airstrip and the weather must be perfect for the plane to land and take off. One day of poor weather and the passengers get bumped to the next day's flight. There had been no flights for two days to Skardu and everything was badly overbooked. To get us on the next plane, nine passengers with reservations would have to wait yet another day. That proved too big a hurdle for the manager and our principles. Also, Steve and I were informed that our equipment, which had swelled in Islamabad to 1,700 kilograms, could only be sent piece by piece as cargo space became available. The time frame required to accomplish that task seemed to be anyone's guess.

We decided to take the bus.

Simple as that sounds, the bus journey from Islamabad to Skardu is not to be undertaken lightly. Phil said, "Taking the bus is a great way to get to Skardu . . . once." Ours would be Phil's fifth trip. The Karakoram Highway follows caravan routes of the Old Silk Road from China to Persia along the Indus River. The road is both a spectacular and frightening feat of engineering.

Nazir Sabir arranged a private bus for our team. We left Islamabad late in the afternoon of May 26, driving out of town amid an environmentalist's purgatory of the choking diesel fumes and blaring horns which haunt third world traffic jams. The fumes are a result of low grade fuel and trucks which still run, but only just. The constant blasting of horns must in some way satisfy the drivers who feel that such a bothersome noise will surely speed up the snarled traffic on overcrowded roads.

It was 5:30 PM and the day was still a sizzling hot 45 degrees celsius.

Every square inch of our bus was decorated. Religious trinkets, every colour of paint, shiny baubles, bells and stickers were lashed, stuck, taped or stencilled in every conceivable spot on our "magic carpet" to Skardu. Most of the buses we saw travelling the rough roads to northern Pakistan were similarly adorned, a display of the owner's pride in their possession. Fortunately, ours was a sturdy vehicle with reliable tires and a new diesel engine, because the journey was long and gruelling. As we requested, our bus came with three drivers. Little did we know one man would do all of the driving while the other two would simply provide the sole driver with shoulder massages and change the cassettes in the tape deck. The poorly recorded, high-pitched Islamic songs blasting through the scratchy speakers in our bus added an annoying twist to the general din of our exit out of the city.

As we escaped the crowds of Islamabad and headed north on the highway, the sun dipped below the horizon. With the darkness came cooler night air flowing through the open windows of the bus, a refreshing change from the daytime heat. Somewhere on the road in central Pakistan we stopped to eat at a truck stop, a noisy and dirty concrete building crowded with men trying to eat and watch the small black and white television in the corner of the restaurant. Most had an unkempt look and stared curiously at us as we sat down at a table in the corner.

After several hours on the road, our most essential need was a bathroom. The only toilet was through a door in the back of the restaurant to a junkyard full of old tires and broken down trucks. It was a simple hole through a slab of concrete and there was no ladies room. Pakistan is an Islamic country and because of strong religious beliefs, women are seldom seen in public. Stacy used the same toilet hole we did. Dinner was the standard fare of dal and chapatti — spiced lentils and flat bread. There was no choice, no *"à la carte"* on the menu. It was eat or go hungry. We all ate. Immediately after a dinner that had us all wondering what antibiotics were in the team's medical kit, we settled back in our bus and tried to sleep while the kilometres rumbled away beneath us. Doctor John passed out sleeping pills to those who wanted them. I put on my headphones, switched on my choice of music, Dire Straits, and stared out into the darkness.

The night passed slowly and without comfort. Our bus had been modified to accommodate forty-four passengers, and to accomplish that in a relatively small vehicle, the seats were bolted to the floor leaving an absolute minimum of space for a pair of legs. With all of our gear piled to the ceiling at the back and in the aisle, there was not enough room to stretch out. To add to the discomfort, the bus's suspension was brutally stiff and transferred every jarring pothole through my back and up to my unsupported head. Any bit of sleep I managed was roughly interrupted before it got near the point of being restful. Ghulam sat up through the night. He dozed occasionally but mostly just sat quietly — resigned, almost content.

When daylight finally arrived we had been driving for twelve hours, and I became aware that the darkness had provided a sense of security. Our bus had been winding its way along a dirt track etched in the side of the gorge of the raging Indus River. An insignificant line on a wall of rock. It was immediately clear that no road

The colourful paint and decorations on the bus we hired are a common characteristic of the vehicles which drive to Pakistan's northern districts. Our bus also had sturdy tires, a powerful diesel engine and strong suspension. Low gear ratios enabled our driver to move slowly but confidently around difficult corners and up steep hills in his heavily loaded bus. Transportation along the rugged Karakoram Highway is largely restricted to this style of stout trucks and buses.

The road from Islamabad to Skardu follows the route of the old Silk Road from Persia to China. During our epic bus ride from Islamabad to Skardu we stopped to stretch our legs and view these rock carvings of ibex and other symbols.

was meant to be where we were and that the term highway was a complete misnomer. Below the "highway" was the raging torrent of a determined river which, over the centuries, has carved its way through the Himalayas. Above were peaks which soared for thousands of metres to the sky.

Continually beset by rockfall and landslides from earth tremors and torrential rains, the Karakoram Highway has opened the northern districts of Pakistan. The traditional route through Srinagar was closed in 1947 when Pakistan received its independence but lost control of the Kashmir district to India. The new road is an excellent route to observe geology in action but unfortunately is often closed for days, weeks or even months for repair. Whatever engineers scheme, it seems nature will always dictate whether Pakistan's lifeline to the north is open or closed.

For hours we travelled along this treacherous road barely wider than our bus. If traffic had been coming the other way one of the vehicles would have been required to back up to one of the all-too-few spots used as pull-outs. There were hundreds, perhaps thousands, of completely blind corners where our driver would sound the horn and creep slowly around the curve. At one point, our roof scraped the rock wall on one side and I heard Dan's cry of fear from the other side as he looked directly into the powerful, crashing turbulence of the Indus River, hundreds of metres below. Any driver error, any vehicle breakdown – a tire puncture, a brake failure, a broken pin in the steering mechanism – any one of these problems could have sent the bus over the edge.

In Islam they say, "Insha' Allah" – if Allah wills it – and many things in Pakistan which are beyond one's means or control are simply reasoned in the spirit of that philosophy. I hoped that our driver and his bus had an attitude of practical survival and not only a religious philosophy.

After twenty-eight straight hours on the road, all with the same tired driver, we pulled safely into Skardu just at nightfall on May 27. Every one of us swore we would fly back to Islamabad after our climb was over, regardless of the cost. The risk seemed too great to take a chance on the bus again. Doctor John was adamant and gestured wildly with his arms, telling us in colourful terms that he would never ride the Karakoram Highway again. Phil had just finished his fifth trip and each time he had claimed it would be his last. I hoped to fly on the way home, but knew that sometimes you do what has to be done. Even in retrospect, the journey along that road seems the most dangerous part of our trip, the time when I felt least in control.

Despite the terrifying bus ride, our journey to K2 was going well. Every step of the way things seemed to be working out in our favour. The team was feeling positive. In some ways we created success with our effort and in other respects we were

A quick snapshot from our moving bus shows the Karakoram Highway and its perilous track on the side of the Indus River gorge. Completed in 1979, the highway was primarily built for strategic purposes. 500 workers died during its construction over 20 years.

Muhammad Ali, Ghulam's close friend and helper, was a tireless worker who became an important part of our team. One of his jobs in Base Camp was to carry the many gallons of cooking and drinking water we needed from an icy melt-water river running on top of the Godwin-Austen Glacier to the kitchen. Ghulam ensured that every team on the Strip collected their drinking water from the same side of the moraine, using the other side for a toilet.

simply lucky. As I settled into my bed that evening at the K2 Hotel, very tired and anxious to catch up on the previous night's lost sleep, rain began to fall. Before long thunder sounded and big drops of water bounced loudly off the tin roof. It was 10:00 PM. I listened as the storm's cadence developed a regular beat and became more aware of the faint, ceaseless creaking of the spinning fan on the ceiling. Although irritated at first, I comforted myself with thoughts of how dangerous it would be on the Karakoram Highway in this kind of a storm. I was happy to be where I was.

We had been off the road for only three hours when the downpour struck. That night, only one kilometre past Skardu, the highway we had yet to travel was buried under two metres of mud and debris. The slide was over 500 metres wide.

Insha' Allah.

THE MORNING OF MAY 28 dawned clear and fresh. The air was cool and the views of the mountains were inspiring. After days of travel, overwhelming heat and bureaucratic paper-shuffling in Islamabad, it was invigorating to breathe clean mountain air and see new snow on the foothills of the Karakoram Mountains. Joining us that morning was the final member of our expedition, Muhammad Ali, the son of Ibrahim — Ghulam's close friend. Muhammad was a fine addition to our team, cheerfully and tirelessly helping with cooking and camp chores.

Despite the beautiful morning and the relaxing social atmosphere, we still had many chores to accomplish before leaving Skardu. Enjoying the sunshine, we ate a breakfast of toast, eggs and fruit on the green lawn of the courtyard at the K2 Hotel and split up the day's responsibilities.

Skardu bustles. A town of about 30,000 people, it is the administrative centre of Baltistan, a large region in Northern Pakistan. The focus of Skardu is commerce. People from outlying areas bring their goods for trade while supplies from the south and from China to the north arrive by truck on days that an open road allows.

Dan and I had spent the previous year organizing the expedition's food and menu, so it seemed logical that we do the final shop in Skardu before our journey into the mountains. We set off with Ghulam after breakfast carrying several thick wads of rupees to buy food and supplies.

Trying to keep up with Ghulam in the streets of Skardu was not easy. His pace was brisk and I was distracted by the colourful visual scenes and the bustle of the marketplace. The smells of the many spices and streetside restaurants were alluring. I was continually being distracted, but Ghulam was all business. We followed him down narrow alleyways, past scores of shops and stalls and deep into the heart of

The sights, sounds and smells of the Skardu marketplace were fascinating. Spices, vegetables, nuts, fruit, pots, pans, flour, tea, coffee — anything necessary to live in northern Pakistan — could be found there. Chickens are weighed and sold alive because refrigeration is a luxury that few homes can afford.

← PREVIOUS LEAF

Ghulam shops for nuts and dried fruit in Skardu. He purchased everything our team needed for three months on the glacier, including food and supplies for our 104 porters, from a list in his head, and accomplished the task in a single day.

Skardu's market area as he bartered with shopkeepers and calculated what supplies were needed. Ghulam was shopping not only for our team but also for the one hundred or more porters we would soon be hiring to carry our food and equipment to Base Camp — a journey of eight or more days.

Dan and I followed Ghulam all day, obediently paying various shopkeepers vast sums of rupees. We left each shop having shared chai, a sweet milky tea, with the owner of the stall, and having been partially relieved of our heavy weight of money. At the end of the day we hired two small trucks and returned to each shop for the packaged merchandise. As we rolled back to the hotel, our trucks were loaded with over 800 kilograms of flour, stoves, kerosene, nuts, rice, tea, matches, kitchen utensils, lanterns, sugar, spices, pots, water containers, dried fruit, milk, lentils, salt, cigarettes for the porters and assorted other items deemed necessary by Ghulam for our K2 adventure.

We gathered all of our purchases in the courtyard of the K2 Hotel just after sunset. Our next chore was to make thirty or so porter loads, each weighing twenty-five kilograms. It could have waited until the next morning, but Dan insisted we continue working into the evening to maintain our momentum toward the mountain. There was some grumbling by team members about the late hour and the fact that everyone had been busy all day, but this tension was merely the product of fatigue and personality differences that lasted only a few minutes.

The worst job was flour re-packaging. John Haigh had just arrived in the courtyard after showering and changing into clean clothes. As was his style, he jumped at the task and before long he was converting the large sacks of flour into waterproof, porter-size loads. We had bought 480 kilograms of wheat flour, and by the time there were nineteen bags stacked neatly against the wall of our storage room, John looked like a ghost from an old black and white movie. His beard and hair were dusty white and his shoes were full of flour, but the job was done. We were ready for the final mechanically assisted leg of our journey by jeep the following morning to Askole.

It was a week since we had left Seattle. We had all the supplies we needed and were only a single day's drive from the trailhead. Team spirit was high and there was a strong sense of purpose. In anticipation of at least two months in the mountains, we ate our final restaurant dinner then gathered in John Haigh's room and secretively shared a shot or two of scotch. Pakistan is a strict Muslim country where alcohol is forbidden. We talked and laughed well into the night.

Before leaving the following morning we began the process of hiring the porters we would need to get our 2500 kilograms of food and gear in to the mountain. Our chief porter, or *Sirdar*, Ali Hussein, wanted to employ as many men as possible from Skardu, his home town. Stacy and Yousaf, together with Ali, chose thirty porters from the hundred or more men who had gathered at the gate of the K2 Hotel looking for work. Once hired, it was each man's responsibility to reach Askole by the next day to begin the trek to K2. At least twenty of our newly hired porters rented a jeep and piled inside for the rugged trip, while others jumped on the top of one of our five, fully-loaded jeeps as our caravan began the drive to Askole.

The route out of Skardu wanders eighty kilometres to Dasso. Except for half a kilometre of extremely rough travel across the recent landslide just out of town, it was a well maintained gravel road. The main village along the way is Shigar, a lush town full of flowers and apricot trees. An oasis amid the dry rocks and dust of the low mountains, Shigar's abundance is the result of centuries of work building kilometres of irrigation ditches which channel water from distant mountain streams to the village. We stopped in the shade of the town's apricot trees to stretch and make our required visit to the police station. We had just entered a new district and Stacy had yet another stack of forms to complete.

In Shigar Phil was re-united with Ahmat, his friend and porter from two previous trips into the Karakoram. Somehow, by keeping his ear to the ground, Ahmat had learned that Phil was returning to Pakistan to climb K2. He brought ten companions to Shigar expecting to work for our expedition. A conflict arose when the local Shigar administrator wanted his men hired, not Ahmat's crew. He had the power to tie up our expedition in Shigar for days with bureaucracy if he chose. Yousaf stepped forward and spoke with the village elder. After forty minutes of deliberation over a cup of chai, Ahmat and his friends joined us as we pulled out of Shigar for Dasso.

From Dasso to Askole, the road follows the Braldu River gorge for forty kilometres, reviving our recent memories of the Karakoram Highway. It took four dangerous hours of bouncing precariously around hairpin corners in low range four-wheel drive and crossing the brown, mud-filled torrent of the Braldu on cable suspension bridges one jeep at a time — the dangling span swaying in the wind — to reach Askole. My knuckles were white from gripping the seat in front of me, and it was a relief to know the mechanized portion of our approach was behind us.

From Askole to K2 Base Camp was an eight to ten day trek along trails beneath grand mountains and across wide glaciers. It would provide a chance for us to focus on the mountain we had travelled around the world to climb. We set up our tents in a blustery, evening wind storm on a green field below the village. Dinner consisted of tinned gourmet chili from Washington and was our first North American meal in a week. After eating, we walked up the hill to Askole to purchase the final portion of our porters' provisions — the meat ration.

Men came from villages several kilometres away to find work with our expedition. The job would take them away from their families for ten or more days to carry heavy loads using wretched suspension systems and would take them high into the cold mountains. Most were poorly equipped, using wool blankets at 5000 metres to keep warm and cheap shoes unable to provide protection or support. The pay we offered was $6.50 a day. Despite such poor work options, our team had our choice of the strongest men from the several hundred vying for employment.

Before I left Askole I purchased this small prayer charm from a young girl in the village for ten rupees — about thirty-five cents. I strapped it on my pack for good luck and it remained there for the entire trip.

It was nearly dusk as we were led through the ancient alleyways of Askole, past one of the village's new water taps — made possible by gifts from climbers and the region's historical leader, the Aga Khan, all organized by British mountaineer, Doug Scott — and down dirt steps to the home of Haji Mehdi, the leader of the tribes of the Braldu valley. The houses in Askole are better defined as smoke-blackened huts. They are built of stone, timber and mud-bricks with thatched stick roofs and often a large room in the basement for livestock. The people of Askole are herders and they keep their goats and cows within the walls of the village at night for protection from poachers, dogs, or an unlikely attack by the rare and endangered snow leopard.

Yousaf and Ali Hussein spoke in Balti with the locals and motioned for us to enter through a small wooden door. Inside the light was dim but revealed a room with a low ceiling and a collection of assorted chairs around a small table in the centre. The room had that musty, third world scent — a blend of smoke, animals and humans. It is a distinct and bitter odour that I never quite get used to. There was one small window which let in the dying light of the day. The door closed behind us and we sat in the near-dark and waited.

Moments later, led by two men bearing modern kerosene lanterns, Haji Mehdi entered the room. We were sitting in folding deck chairs, leftover equipment from the dozens of expeditions which pass through town. Except for these few minor props from the twentieth century, the scene could have taken place several hundred years ago. Greetings were exchanged and in a hushed manner Stacy's presence was questioned. It is unusual in rural Pakistan for women to be involved in such rituals and with business dealings. Yousaf explained that she was our leader. After that I am certain the character of the rest of us, as male members of our team, was silently questioned.

Before any business could be discussed the ritual of chai had to be observed. The sweet tea mixture, very heavy on the sugar and milk, came on a rough tray in as many different styles of cups as there were people. When a bowl of hard-boiled eggs was passed around the room, the man's hands rough and soiled — black dirt trapped under each fingernail after a lifetime of working the fields around Askole — I graciously declined the offer and sipped chai hesitantly from my dirty cup.

Once the ceremony was over and the mandatory exchanges in Balti concluded, the bargaining began. Each side expressed their needs: our K2 team would require meat and Haji Mehdi wanted money. It was well after dark and we were taken to black, unlit basements in opposite corners of Askole to look at goats and then a dso — a cross between a cow and an ox. The goats are considered a delicacy by the porters but are expensive. The dso was a great beast with a huge head and broad horns. It weighed 200 kilograms. We opted for the dso and paid Haji Mehdi $250

Dan walks through the village of Askole stopping to chat with a curious resident. Mud brick and stone homes with thatched roofs provide shelter for the local Balti herdsmen.

The paperwork required by the government of Pakistan was a bit overwhelming at times. Each porter employed by our expedition signed a contract by way of a thumbprint. Once employed, each man received his twenty-five kilogram load to carry and was automatically covered by an insurance policy we were obliged to purchase for them. On hiring day, Stacy and Yousaf managed to stay organized despite the stack of forms and hundreds of men competing for work.

RIGHT

This porter waited patiently for his name to be called hoping his experience would get him work before the horde of younger men who had gathered looking for a chance to join our expedition to K2 Base Camp.

for our porters' meat ration. The animal would accompany our expedition to the toe of the Baltoro Glacier where it would be slaughtered and eaten on the porters' rest day.

After the deal was struck, we wound our way through the dark narrow lanes of Askole and walked back into camp and our twentieth century.

I crawled into my sleeping bag for the first time on the trip and closed the zipper as the evening air was quickly cooling. It felt good to be lying in a tent; it gave me the sense of being in the mountains. Sleep came easily.

May 30 was our porter hiring day and they came out in force. Several hundred men arrived at our camp, each hoping to be one of the one hundred or more porters we would eventually employ. Yousaf, Stacy and Ali Hussein managed the hiring process while Doctor John inspected each potential porter for any obvious health problems. Dan and I took photographs. John Petroske and Steve watched in fascination at the process of hiring this man's cousin or that man's brother. In each instance, our team was promised in rough and broken English that this friend was "a good man" or "a strong porter." Even in Askole, one needs to network to get a job.

Ultimately accompanying the seven of us on our journey to K2 Base Camp were 104 porters, two sirdars, two cooks, one liaison officer and one ill-fated 200 kilogram dso.

W E B E G A N T H E A P P R O A C H trek at noon on May 30 and joined the trail to K2 Base Camp through the narrow lanes defined by the primitive homes in Askole. We were on our way. The trail followed the Braldu River and we slowly climbed up the valley and camped at the traditional site of Korophon Tsok — Balti for *Big Rock and Thorns.* On that first day we had been forced to cross the Biafo Glacier as its snout pushed right into our path — a left turn on that glacier would take an expedition to the Latok Peaks, The Ogre or one of many unclimbed rock spires. The Biafo valley contains some of the most difficult climbing in the Karakoram. When we pitched our tents that first night on the trail I was already dreaming of and calculating my next adventure. Phil told me stories of his trips to Latok III and Lukipilla Brak, hard routes only two days away from our campsite.

We left camp early the following morning. The trail crosses the Dumordu River which flows from the Panmah Glacier, but the cable car normally used to reach the other side of the main channel of the Dumordu had been washed out by flooding. Our porters were eager to ford the cold river before the heat of the day caused the water level to rise. We crossed where the river had formed a series of channels. The many arteries made for easier wading and reduced the danger of

We arrived in Pakistan with specialized backpacks utilizing high-tech suspension systems and lightweight material. Our porters relied on hemp ropes and leather thongs to lash our heavy loads to their backs.

someone stumbling and losing a load. I wondered what I would do if the bag containing my climbing boots was lost to the muddy stream, but the porters barely broke stride as they reached the water. Most of them peeled off their shoes to keep them dry and made short work of the crossing, showing little sign of discomfort.

Dan tried to follow the example of our porters and removed his hiking boots but quickly realized that his feet did not have the same leather-like callouses as our Balti helpers. I passed Dan, moving across the unseen bottom rocks more quickly in shoes, even though my feet were completely numb from the glacial water. The rest of the team opted to wear shoes or sandals as well. I waited for Dan on the far side and watched with empathy as he gingerly took each step in the freezing river. When he reached the east side of the Dumordu, Dan told me he had been close to losing consciousness from the icy pain in his feet. I wrung out my socks and sloshed up the trail, happy to have wet shoes after hearing Dan's tale of suffering.

The way to K2 is divided into stages for the purpose of paying porters. They get paid for each stage that they carry a load. There are twelve stages on the route, but usually the trip is accomplished in seven or eight days. Our approach trek took eight days including a rest day at Paiju.

We reached Paiju campsite, a height of 3500 metres, on the afternoon of the third day. The clouds were low, there was a light wind blowing and a misty rain chilled the air. Despite the drizzle, the ground was dry and dusty. The toilet for the hundreds of people who pass through Paiju was simply the hillside below camp. Countless piles of faeces were scattered everywhere and soiled toilet paper was carried in the wind. Under every rock there was human waste. It was revolting. Doctor John was so appalled by the disgusting conditions at Paiju he felt certain some of us would become sick from the filth of the place. He made sure that each of us, especially Ghulam and Muhammud Ali, washed our hands in a mixture of water and bleach before handling any food. Despite these precautions, John sensed that sickness was inevitable. Later in the trip, Stacy had intestinal problems and Steve was weakened by a virus, and while it is impossible to know if they developed their ailments at Paiju, that campsite was indisputably foul.

I had never been associated with a big Himalayan expedition. In fact, I had never been to the Himalayas and while I was impressed with the size of our undertaking, I was concerned about its impact on the environment. That concern was reinforced throughout our trip by the garbage and faeces left everywhere by climbing expeditions and trekking parties. The thousands of porters who carry loads into the Karakoram use the drinking water streams and their banks as toilets, conveniently washing their hands after wiping. The worst offender of all has been the Pakistan military. Stationed strategically at both Paiju and Concordia to support the supply

THE HEART
OF THE
KARAKORAM

Our approach from Askole to K2 Base Camp took eight days. We travelled through the Baltoro Corridor beneath some of the world's greatest peaks. Our expedition was accompanied by 104 porters, two cooks, one liaison officer and one large dso.

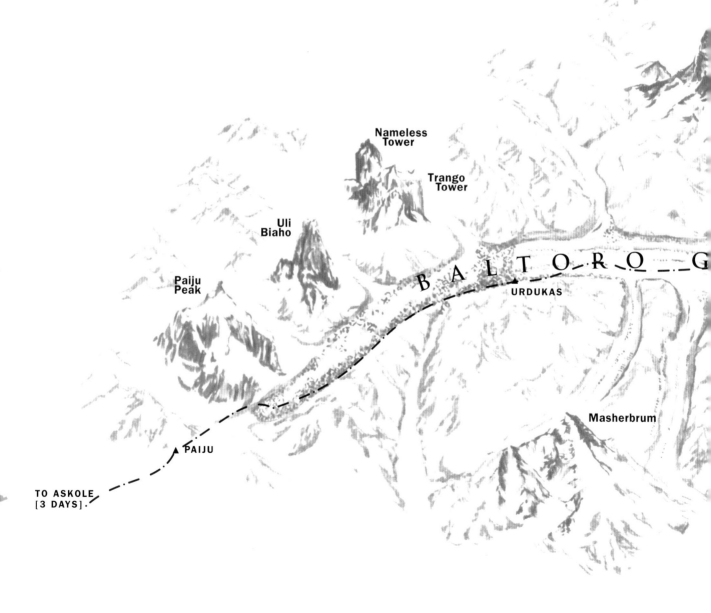

Nameless Tower

Trango Tower

Uli Biaho

Paiju Peak

BALTORO G

URDUKAS

Masherbrum

PAIJU

TO ASKOLE
[3 DAYS]

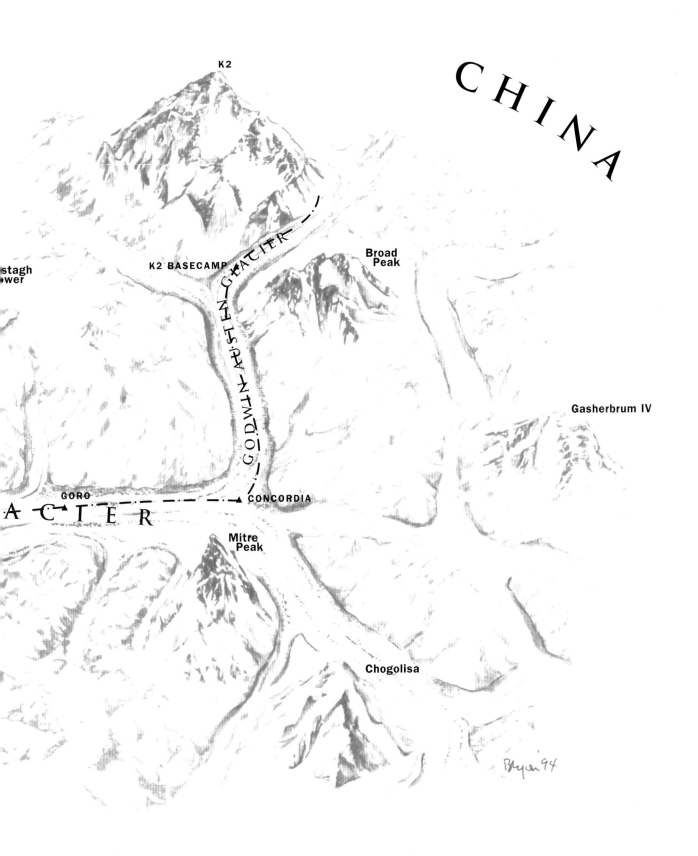

The garbage left by other expeditions at K2 Base Camp is a sad legacy for mountaineers. Burnt batteries, broken glass, melted plastic and thousands of rusty tins combine to create a disgusting mess among the rocks and ice of the Godwin Austen Glacier.

line to the Siachen Glacier area where the highest war in the world is waged with India — they only fight in the relative warmth of the summer — the army camps have literally trashed the place. There has been little thought of the environmental consequences of their presence. Mountains of tins, spent fuel canisters, dead animals left to rot on the glacier and garbage scattered across the Karakoram are a daily part of trekking along the Baltoro Corridor.

The Karakoram mountains are among the most spectacular on Earth, but the filth of human influence has tarnished the Baltoro Glacier and the surrounding peaks like salt air on brass fittings. It will take years of dedication and education to clean and restore the area to its natural state.

Before we left K2, our team collected over 500 kilograms of garbage around Base Camp. We burned what we could, tossing the ashes down a deep crevasse in the glacier, and paid for porters to carry the remainder, over 250 kilograms of plastic, spent batteries and tins, out to Skardu. We did not even scratch the surface of a growing problem.

Paiju is the final stop before the Baltoro Glacier, so the porters usually spend an extra rest day there and bake bread in anticipation of spending the next four or five nights on the glacier where there is no wood. At Paiju we got our first glimpses of the great Karakoram Peaks. As afternoon passed into evening, the skies cleared and the clean air following the storm produced a spectacular sunset on the Trango Towers and other unnamed summits to the south. The moon rose brightly near Masherbrum. Despite the shocking pollution, the Karakoram magic was taking hold.

Our rest day at Paiju on June 2 was warm and sunny, so we took the opportunity for a cold bath in the Biaho River which flows out from under the Baltoro Glacier — two kilometres away. That brisk wash was our last for eight weeks using running water. Later that day, the dso was slaughtered by Ali Hussein wielding a knife that really needed some attention on a good whetstone and our porters enjoyed their entire seven day meat ration in one gluttonous feast.

As it turned out, the butchering of the dso and the porters' rest day coincided with the Islamic holiday Eid-ul-Zuha, a kind of Christmas-like occasion which celebrates Abraham's willingness to sacrifice his son Isaac to God. The way the story goes in Islam is that at the last instant God replaced Isaac with a goat. Today, the locals commemorate Abraham's act of faith by bleeding to death whatever animal they can afford — be it goat, cow, or chicken — with a slice to the throat. Our porters enjoyed the festivities while I conscientiously photographed the dso slaying and considered becoming a vegetarian. For dinner that evening, however, Ghulam prepared a curried dish with fresh meat he had been given by the porters; despite our winces and flinching earlier in the day as most of us watched the dso being slowly

RIGHT

As we trekked further into the mountains the days got colder and afternoon snow showers were common. This porter works his way toward Urdukas at 4100 metres in plastic shoes with no socks.

killed, each of us ate the tasty meal with our usual relish.

The next day we embarked on the final four days of our approach trek with newly satiated porters. I marvelled at their outward contentment considering the rough terrain and their various forms of inappropriate footwear ranging from plastic running shoes to old leather walking boots falling apart at the seams. We walked along beside them wearing the latest equipment from North America and carrying our light daypacks complete with high-tech suspension systems. Meanwhile, the porters carried loads which included twenty-five kilograms of our supplies and five or so additional kilos of their own gear strapped somewhere on top. I wondered how they managed the weight as the few bits of rope or leather thongs they used for straps pressed deeply into the flesh on their shoulders.

The Baltoro Glacier is the main thoroughfare to the heart of the Karakoram mountains. Three days of walking took us past peaks which would provide a lifetime of climbing for any mountaineer: Paiju Peak, Uli Biaho, Trango Towers, Nameless Tower, Masherbrum, Baltoro Cathedral, Lobsang Spire, Mustagh Tower and numerous unclimbed summits, faces and rock walls, many unnamed, to a spectacular camp at the meeting of the Baltoro and Godwin-Austen Glaciers — Concordia. I came to these mountains a seasoned mountaineer and professional mountain guide, yet I found myself as genuinely excited as a small child at Christmas. These were the world's greatest peaks and I was walking among them; unbelievably, I was bound for K2, the greatest mountain of all.

Concordia is in the centre of the Karakoram and only a day's trek from K2 Base Camp. When we arrived the winter snow still covered the glacier and I had a sense that we had stepped from the foothills into the big mountains. We had reached the high alpine. For me it was what I had travelled around the world to see; for the porters it was a difficult time. They were poorly equipped for snow and cold temperatures; to them, enjoying the awesome beauty of Concordia was secondary to staying warm and simply surviving.

We were camped at 4500 metres and the night-time temperature dipped to -10 degrees celsius. Each porter carried only one blanket. To keep warm at night, groups of men would gather in village or family units and place several blankets on the rocks, lie down together and draw the remaining blankets over top of the entire group. Above them was a plastic tarpaulin, propped up with a simple walking stick to form a roof. Like sardines in a tin, our Balti porters nestled together for warmth in the high mountain camp at Concordia. Twenty-five metres away, each member of our team slept comfortably inside tents and goose-down sleeping bags on insulated pads.

The normal justification for this inequality is that we offer our porters the best work available in the area and each man we hired was happy that we had chosen

him. The contract we shared with each individual stated that he was responsible for his own equipment. We paid each a gear allowance of 150 rupees for that purpose. Almost without exception, that stipend went straight to their family before we left, not to obtain better equipment for the trek. It is a world where many things are difficult to understand. They were the Balti porters and we were the "wealthy" North American climbers. We had come to scare ourselves on a mountain that clearly broadcasts a message through ghastly weather conditions, high altitude and a long history of tragedy to stay off its ridges and faces. I am certain they thought we were the fools, and it would be difficult to argue with them.

On the final leg of our approach from Concordia to K2 we were blessed with a perfect day; the skies cleared completely and the steep mass of the mountain we had come to attempt shot high into the crystalline, blue air of the Himalayas.

K2 dominates.

It is a mountain of dreams that gives away nothing in reality. I hurried through two rolls of film, fumbling with cold fingers trying to ensure that I had at least one classic shot of the peak. It was an exhilarating place to be at that moment, a moment when we all realized, each in our own way, what lay clearly in front of us. This was no picture in a book. The wind on the ridges at 8000 metres and the fresh snow blanketing the 3500 metre South Face were very real. I shivered inside and contemplated cold feet, headaches and sleepless nights high on the mountain. After those thoughts I solemnly put my camera away and continued the trek up the glacier toward Base Camp.

We had reached K2.

Ultraviolet, infrared and visible light are dangerous hazards which are magnified by the snow and high altitude. Mountaineers use dark sunglasses which filter out harmful rays. Some of our porters did not have sunglasses and to help protect their eyes we fashioned these narrow-slit shields out of duct tape.

← PREVIOUS LEAF

Concordia is the meeting of the Baltoro and Godwin-Austen Glaciers at 4600 metres. Our porters cluster together to socialize and to keep warm. They slept in large groups under plastic tarpaulins while each of us had our own tent to escape to or we could hide from the sun or wind in the expedition's large dining tent. In the background, K2 attempts to shed its veil of clouds – the summit pyramid barely visible.

LEFT

Gasherbrum means "shining wall" and there are few mountain walls in the world to compare with the striking West Face of Gasherbrum IV. With its technically unrelenting and steep terrain, difficult approaches and a summit only 75 metres below the elusive 8000 metre mark, Gasherbrum IV is one of the world's greatest alpine challenges.

K 2 — D R E A M S   A N D   R E A L I T Y

We arrived at K2 Base Camp on June 6, walking toward the mountain on the perfect approach day. The great South Face of K2 dominated like no other mountain I had ever seen; the classic pyramid of the peak we had come to climb soared unchallenged into the crystalline blue sky of the Karakoram.

K2—THE ABRUZZI RIDGE

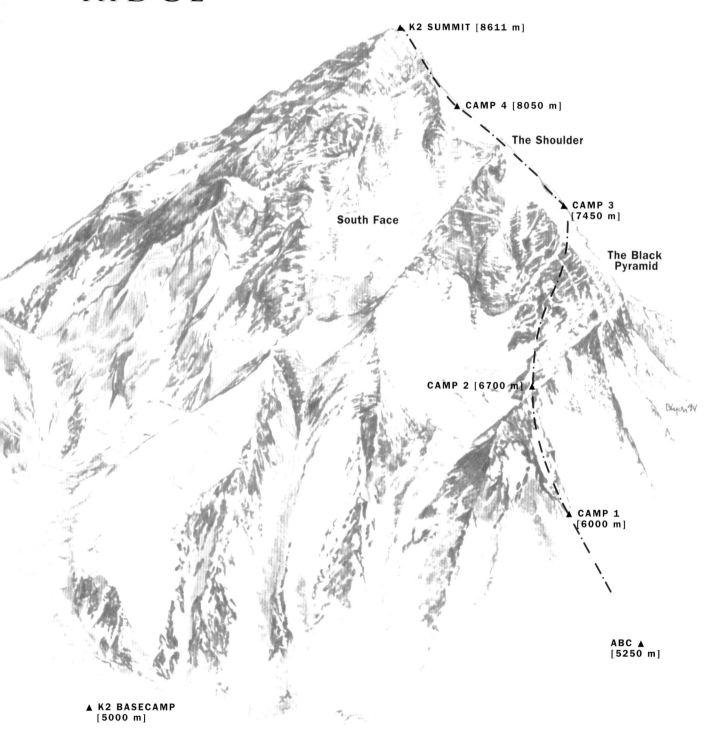

▲ K2 SUMMIT [8611 m]

▲ CAMP 4 [8050 m]

The Shoulder

South Face

▲ CAMP 3 [7450 m]

The Black Pyramid

CAMP 2 [6700 m] ▲

▲ CAMP 1 [6000 m]

ABC ▲ [5250 m]

▲ K2 BASECAMP [5000 m]

IT WAS JUNE 6 and the preparations, formalities, customs, porters, transportation, politics and regulations were behind us. All that remained was to climb the mountain. In some ways that task would be much easier for us. I was anxious to get on with the work at hand but cautious and aware of the need to go slowly and adapt.

We had more than two months left to climb K2. We might need that time to acclimatize to the incredible heights and to wait for the four or five day break of good weather needed to reach the summit from Base Camp. The more time we allowed for both of these critical factors, the more likely we were to succeed. Patience was sure to be a key to reaching our goals.

When we arrived, Base Camp seemed clean and fresh, covered in a new coat of snow. We paid our porters for their twelve stages of work, 180 rupees per stage or about $6.50. A total of less than $80 per man for their eight days of arduous labour on our behalf. They spent no time admiring the grandeur of famous mountains which surrounded our Base Camp at K2: Broad Peak, Chogolisa, The Angelus and the huge South Face of K2 itself. The snow on the ground was cooling their feet and even in the middle of the day the air temperature hovered near freezing. They raced down the glacier to the greening valleys, none wanting to spend a second night at Concordia.

We set our Base Camp at 5000 metres on a broad moraine in the glacier which runs along the base of the South Face of K2, commonly known as "the Strip." The most important decision was which side of the moraine we would use for our drinking water and which side for our toilet. About ten minutes further up the moraine was a large Slovenian-organized international expedition which had already been at Base Camp for two weeks. Ghulam ensured our water was gathered from the same side of the moraine as theirs. Seven expeditions would follow us to K2 that summer – hygiene in Base Camp is critical to success on the mountain.

On Stacy's orders, we impatiently waited out a sunny day in Base Camp to acclimatize. We passed the day building tent platforms and helping move rocks to build Ghulam's kitchen. With each large boulder, Ghulam would say, "Okay. Thank you. Now you rest, I build kitchen." To create the sturdy walls for their kitchen, Muhammad Ali carried rocks for two days while Ghulam laid each stone with care. They knew that before long their effort would be rewarded. The inevitable storms would come to Base Camp and their rock walls would offer snug protection. Finally, on June 8 the seven of us donned packs filled with equipment and food and set off enthusiastically to Advanced Base Camp. Despite our eagerness, the altitude quickly and decisively toned our stride down to a slow trudge. We humped our loads across the glacier, through the icefall and up the moraine to the

Crevasses are the major hazard on snow-covered glaciers; a fall through an unseen crack in the ice could prove fatal. Our team always travelled roped together through the icefall on the Godwin-Austen Glacier as a precaution against that danger.

Reflecting about the trip on the pages of my journal was a common occurence at night in Base Camp.

toe of the Southeast Ridge – more commonly referred to as the Abruzzi Ridge – the route we had chosen to climb.

First attempted in 1909 by a large Italian expedition, the first trip to the Abruzzi Ridge was led by the famous Luigi Amedeo di Savoia – the Duke of Abruzzi. With several European guides on the Duke's payroll, his expedition reached an impressive height of 6250 metres. For our team, even though we had come totally prepared with modern equipment and clothing, the size of the challenge remained as it had eighty-four years earlier. It was on this day I realized just how physically difficult climbing K2 was going to be.

My first trip to Camp 1, at just over 6000 metres, came on June 11 with Steve. Phil and Dan had carried the previous day while Stacy, John Haigh and John Petroske would carry on June 12. I climbed slowly to the exposed site of our lowest camp on the mountain and even more slowly came to grips with the difficulty of catching my breath. There were two facts which I could not overlook. The first was that our Camp 1 was as high as the summit of Denali in Alaska and though I had reached that peak over ten years earlier, the effects of altitude on that day in 1983 had felt paralysing. The second was that the summit of K2 still soared over 2500 metres into the sky above.

One step at a time. Insha' Allah.

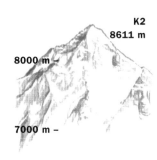

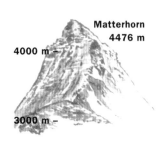

9000 m –

K2
8611 m

8000 m –

7000 m –

Denali
6149 m

6000 m –

5000 m –

Matterhorn
4476 m

4000 m –

3000 m –

2000 m –

1000 m –

0 m – Sea level

OVERLEAF →

Our team leaves Base Camp at sunrise with loads for Camp 1. To ensure easy walking across the Godwin-Austen Glacier, dawn starts on the frozen snow were necessary before the heat of the day made the snowpack too soft to travel on.

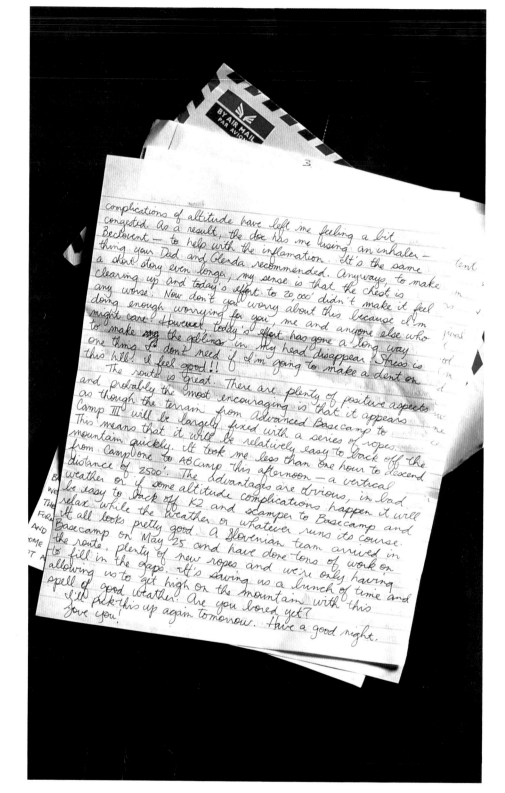

complications of altitude have left me feeling a bit congested. As a result, the doc has me using an inhaler — Beclovent — to help with the inflamation. It's the same thing your Dad and Glenda recommended. Anyways, to make a short story even longer, my sense is that the chest is clearing up and today's effort to 20,000' didn't make it feel any worse. Now don't you worry about this because I'm doing enough worrying for you, me and anyone else who might care. However today's effort has gone a long way to make the gollins in my head disappear. Stress is one thing I don't need if I'm going to make a dent on this hill. I feel good!!

The route is great. There are plenty of positive aspects and probably the most encouraging is that it appears as though the terrain from Advanced Basecamp to Camp III will be largely fixed with a series of ropes. This means that it will be relatively easy to back off the mountain quickly. It took me less than one hour to descend from Camp one to ABCamp this afternoon — a vertical distance of 2500'. The advantages are obvious, in bad weather or if some altitude complications happen it will be easy to back off K2 and scamper to Basecamp and relax while the weather or whatever runs its course. It all looks pretty good. A Slovenian team arrived in Basecamp on May 25 and have done tons of work on the route, plenty of new ropes and we're only having to fill in the gaps. It's saving us a bunch of time and allowing us to get high on the mountain with this spell of good weather. Are you bored yet? I'll pick this up again tomorrow. Have a good night. Love you!

Our many days in Base Camp passed in various ways. I wrote several letters home to my girl-friend sharing with her my thoughts about our expedition.

WEATHER PROVED TO BE our ally in the middle days of June. Everyone on the team worked hard on the mountain and on June 13, Phil and Dan established Camp 2 at 6700 metres, both of them acclimatizing well and carrying heavy loads of fifteen kilograms on their backs. Our second camp was situated just above House's Chimney, a famous section on the Abruzzi Ridge named after Bill House, who pioneered the way through the steep band of rock at that height during an American attempt on K2 in 1938. By reaching Camp 2 after only one week it was clear that the good weather had enabled us to keep a steady schedule up the mountain.

During these days each of us climbed the lower part of the route to Camp 1 several times, leaving our loads and returning to sleep in Base Camp. Ferrying food and equipment up K2 was a tedious but necessary chore. We would need to be acclimatized and well supplied on the mountain in order to make one quick ascent to the top.

I had left North America with some congestion in my chest and I was concerned about going to high altitude with this condition. It kept me low on the mountain initially, and I was careful not to push myself too hard at the start of our climb. Doctor John listened to my breathing with a stethoscope in Base Camp and prescribed a Beclovent inhaler, a steroid, to combat the congestion. I was diligent with the drugs but frustrated with the timing of the problem.

We got our first taste of bad weather on June 14. Storms lashed at the upper mountain, and while we continued shuttling loads on K2's lower slopes, 3000 metres above us the powerful and experienced Slovenian-organized international team was struggling for their lives in Camp 4.

They had quickly established three camps on the mountain though they had trouble maintaining or getting above Camp 3 at 7400 metres due to deep snow and high winds. On June 11, only eighteen days after arriving in Base Camp, Carlos Carsolio of Mexico and Zvonko Pozgaj of Slovenia attempted to climb to Camp 4 at 8000 metres but, stopped by deep snow on the upper mountain, returned to spend an extra night at Camp 3. The train was rolling by this point, however, and with the clear weather it seemed everybody wanted a shot at the top. Carsolio and Pozgaj were joined at 7400 metres by Viki Groselj of Slovenia and Stipe Bozic of Croatia, experienced mountaineers with more than a dozen 8000 metre summits between them. Together the four climbers moved on to establish Camp 4 on June 12 in a two person tent. The following day all four of the climbers in Camp 4 reached the top of K2 in deteriorating weather.

Meanwhile, two more team members continued working their way up the mountain. The arrival of Bostjan Kekec and Boris Sedej of Slovenia increased the

Snow falls from the sky but is affected in numerous ways by temperature, pressure and wind. This sastrugi, or wavelike snow, near Camp 3 is heavily wind blown and compressed, making for very awkward and tiring climbing.

K2 — DREAMS AND REALITY

Dan climbs the steep terrain between Camps 1 and 2 using fixed lines to protect his way.

Swedish climber Daniel Bidner works his way up the rocks and snow above Camp 1 on the Abruzzi Ridge.

pressure on both the small tent and the limited supplies at Camp 4 on the night of June 13. Due to poor weather, Carsolio and Bozic were unable to return to high camp that night; they elected to bivouac in the open, high on K2's slopes, but struggled back from the summit to Camp 4 early in the morning of June 14 in blizzard conditions. Despite extreme fatigue and whiteout conditions, Groselj and Carsolio left immediately for Camp 3 to initiate a rescue for Kekec who was now suffering symptoms of cerebral edema — a deadly affliction caused by high altitude. The body's systems deteriorate and fluid gets trapped in the skull, eventually compressing the brain stem and shutting down the main life support systems located there. Descent is the only treatment.

By noon on June 14, K2 became unforgiving. The climbers still at Camp 4 were trapped in one of the violent assaults of weather for which the mountain is famous.

In a brief window of clear weather on June 15, the four remaining climbers desperately escaped Camp 4. Kekec, however, was unable to move himself at this point and died of cerebral edema somewhere between Camps 4 and 3 as his weakened teammates, dragging his prone body in a sleeping bag, had to abandon him to save themselves. Frostbitten, physically ravaged and emotionally spent, the three remaining climbers trickled back to Base Camp by June 18.

It was a sombre and reflective time on the moraine below K2.

On June 23, another member of the Slovenian team, Goran Kropp of Sweden made the first Swedish ascent of K2 in a bold solo effort from Camp 4. In Base Camp, the population had swelled to more than sixty climbers on seven teams encompassing sixteen nationalities. Everyone was relieved when Kropp managed to find his way off the mountain in worsening weather. Five of the ten members of the Slovenian team had reached the summit in less than four weeks, but the "success" of the expedition was still being hotly debated on the moraine in K2 Base Camp as the single death could have been many had the weather not improved on June 15.

There is a fine line for survival above 8000 metres and it is clear that mountaineers should not use ambition as their sole criterion for decision-making. To reach K2's summit, or any of the world's great peaks, climbers need their share of lucky breaks balanced with patience, good judgement and ability; it seems the more a team or a climber pushes the weather and the mountain, the more they will need to rely on the one factor over which they have no control — luck.

Military helicopters, which supply the Pakistan Army camps at Concordia and Paiju, can act as rescue ambulances for injured climbers. This helicopter landed at K2 Base Camp to pick up two sick and frostbitten Slovenians desperately needing hospital care. Every expedition is required to post a bond or purchase insurance to cover the cost should a helicopter rescue be required.

RIGHT

Dan climbs to Camp 1 in a snow storm.

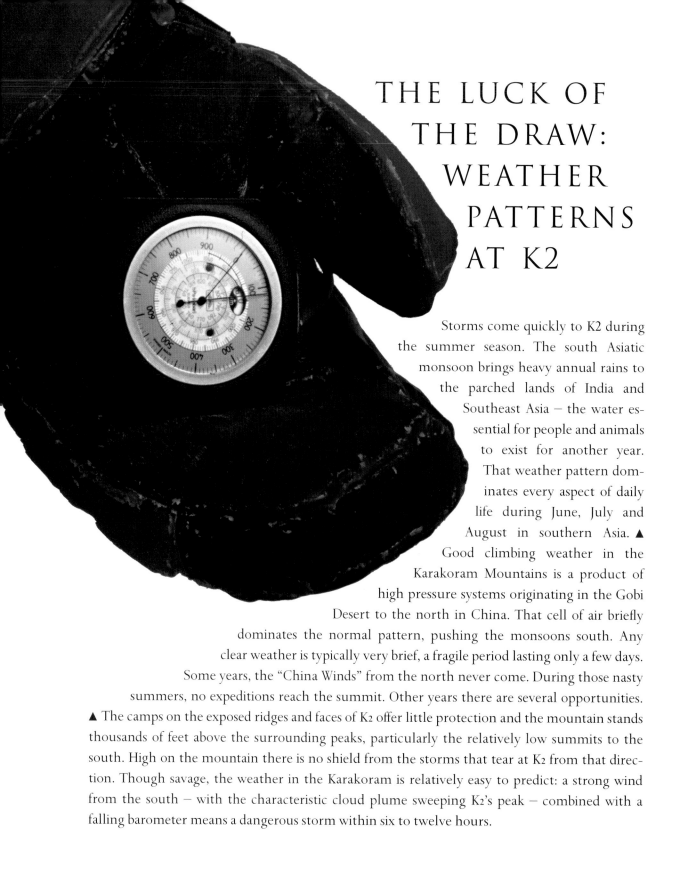

THE LUCK OF THE DRAW: WEATHER PATTERNS AT K2

Storms come quickly to K2 during the summer season. The south Asiatic monsoon brings heavy annual rains to the parched lands of India and Southeast Asia – the water essential for people and animals to exist for another year. That weather pattern dominates every aspect of daily life during June, July and August in southern Asia. ▲ Good climbing weather in the Karakoram Mountains is a product of high pressure systems originating in the Gobi Desert to the north in China. That cell of air briefly dominates the normal pattern, pushing the monsoons south. Any clear weather is typically very brief, a fragile period lasting only a few days. Some years, the "China Winds" from the north never come. During those nasty summers, no expeditions reach the summit. Other years there are several opportunities. ▲ The camps on the exposed ridges and faces of K2 offer little protection and the mountain stands thousands of feet above the surrounding peaks, particularly the relatively low summits to the south. High on the mountain there is no shield from the storms that tear at K2 from that direction. Though savage, the weather in the Karakoram is relatively easy to predict: a strong wind from the south – with the characteristic cloud plume sweeping K2's peak – combined with a falling barometer means a dangerous storm within six to twelve hours.

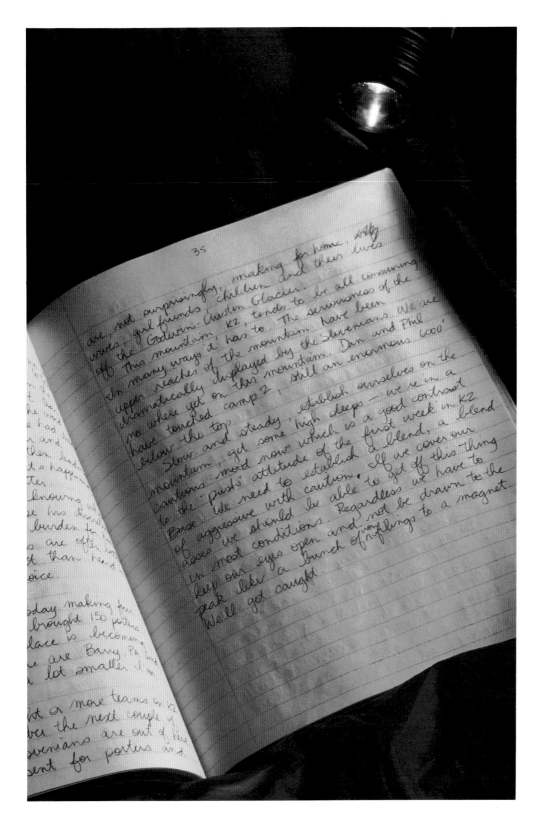

35

are, not surprisingly, making for home, wife, wives, girl friends, children and their lives off. This mountain, K2, tends to be all consuming. In many ways it has to. The seriousness of the upper reaches of the mountain have been dramatically displayed by the Slovenians. We are no where yet on this mountain. Dan and Phil have touched camp 2, still an enormous 6000' below the top.

Slow and steady, establish ourselves on the mountain, get some high sleeps — we're in a cautious mood now which is a good contrast to the "push" attitude of the first week in K2 Base. We need to establish a blend, a blend of aggressive with caution. If we cover our asses we should be able to get off this thing in most conditions. Regardless we have to keep our eyes open and not be drawn to the peak like a bunch of filings to a magnet. We'll get caught.

Pace and patience are important, but subtle, tools necessary to climb a mountain like K2

Dan and Phil try to find a comfortable spot on either side of my feet in the small tent at Camp 2. Despite their happy appearance in this photograph, none of us slept well that night in our crowded shelter. We used down sleeping bags and typically wore most of our clothing each night on the mountain to keep warm.

THE EXCEPTIONAL WEATHER in early June had enabled our team to acclimatize and remain safely ahead of the many other teams which eventually filtered into Base Camp. Of the nine teams at K2, six would concentrate their efforts on the Abruzzi Ridge.

On June 21, Dan, Phil and I climbed from Camp 2 to Camp 3 at 7450 metres through the Black Pyramid, the steepest part of an already steep route. It took us seven gruelling hours to cover the 750 vertical metres and establish a cache of supplies on the broad ridge leading to K2's summit. Tangles of old ropes, left over from years of previous attempts, faded and deteriorated from the sun's intense ultraviolet rays, showed the way. Choosing the best-looking piece of rope from among the many was one of our challenges. The Slovenians had replaced segments of line where they thought it necessary, but had also relied heavily on the ropes which already littered the route. Though protected by fixed lines, we had still to climb the solid rock and kick steps up the steep forty-five degree snow. Through the Black Pyramid the rock was continuously Class 4 with some sheer sections of Class 5 climbing. Each move demanded maximum effort at over 7000 metres.

We all struggled with the altitude but it seemed I was a step behind both Dan and Phil. I considered turning around but knew that it was important to get the gear on my back up the mountain. We were not planning to sleep at Camp 3, so I could get back to Base Camp that night to recover. Dan waited on a rock ledge for me and we shared a drink and a chocolate bar, which seemed to help. Phil was doing most of the trail breaking through the sections of snow and was ahead in the distance.

Near the top of the Black Pyramid I slowed to a crawl and Dan offered to carry part of my load. I had already lost the battle with my pride so I relented and gave him some of the fuel and food that I had in my pack. Phil continued to set the pace and do the hard work in front. Determined and with a substantially lighter pack, I dragged myself to the site of Camp 3.

The descent was remarkably quick as we rappelled to the end of the fixed rope at 5500 metres and then slid down the final 400 metre snowslope on our backsides in only two and half hours. Our planned safety margin seemed to be working well.

The following day, John Haigh and Stacy also made a strong carry to Camp 3, dug a small snow cave and stashed our cache of food and equipment inside. Meanwhile, John Petroske and Steve were working hard and carried for the second time in as many days from Camp 1 to Camp 2. Our climb was going better than expected, and after only fourteen days we were well established on K2's Abruzzi Ridge. Then the second extended storm of our trip hammered into the Karakoram Range and chased us off the mountain.

We spent the next eight days waiting in Base Camp.

Dan stems the icy walls of House's Chimney at 6700 metres just below Camp 2.

CLIMBING STYLE: A MOUNTAINEER'S CHOICES

When we took on the challenge of attempting to reach K2's summit, there were several alternatives in terms of style. How would we choose to climb the mountain? Climbing preferences are very personal and we debated for eighteen months before reaching any conclusions as a team.

Using bottled oxygen on the world's highest peaks is a common practice. At one time it was thought to be necessary above 8000 metres simply to survive. In the tiny cells where oxygen and nutrients are converted to energy and waste products are processed, the body's systems stop functioning properly at very high altitude. Above 7500 metres, evidence suggests that human beings begin to die. Despite this information, mountaineers have successfully climbed to the highest peaks many times without the aid of bottled oxygen. The question is one of style. Do you use oxygen and effectively remove one of the mountain's strongest defences – its height? ▲ Our choice was to attempt the climb without the aid of bottled oxygen. ▲ Another major option a team faces is whether to employ the use of fixed ropes. By establishing permanent ropes on the mountain, a climber is protected from a fall on the ascent by utilizing a mechanical ascender and on the way down by rappelling with a descending device. The alternative is to climb the mountain without leaving any ropes for retreat, belaying steep sections on the way up, setting each rappel as needed on the descent and spending plenty of time to carefully downclimb the route – certainly the more elegant and ambitious style. ▲

K2 is a dangerous mountain. Many climbers have died on its flanks, trapped by fierce storms and unable to descend. Our decision was to leave ropes on parts of the lower mountain where the terrain was continuously steep, steep enough that descent from Camp 3 – at 7450 metres – meant rappelling much of the route. On one of his many trips down the mountain, Phil counted more than ninety rappels from Camp 3 to advanced base camp. The fixed ropes simplified our retreat, enabling us to descend quickly in the event of dangerous weather. Above 7450 metres, we would climb without the aid of fixed lines on the broad ridge that leads to the final summit slopes. ▲ Each team must determine for itself how it will safely climb a mountain. The experience and ability of our team members were the two main factors we considered in reaching our consensus. ▲ Another important decision, whether to leave equipment, ropes and garbage behind, is less a matter of individual choice or style and more a question of responsibility. We are all drawn to the mountains by many things, not the least of which is surely the stunning natural beauty and the personal freedom we associate with mountaineering. By leaving behind evidence of our passage, we diminish the experience for others. K2 is littered with debris from previous attempts and is not alone in a world of polluted mountains. Climbing clean is the only decision that should not be left to choice.

FACING PAGE
A mechanical ascender slides easily then clamps on the rope to prevent a fall.

THIS PAGE
This figure eight descender provides enough friction that a climber can slowly lower down a rope on very steep – even overhanging – terrain

Dan climbs one of the
many vertical rock steps
in the Black Pyramid
between Camps 2 and 3.

Phil's camera captures Dan and me as we move up the fixed ropes in the Black Pyramid. 2000 metres below us are the crevasses of the Godwin-Austen Glacier. From this point there were still 1500 metres of climbing to K2's summit.

Ghulam's rock kitchen was a great place to escape an early morning storm and get a hot mug of chai. Though he could not read any English, Ghulam enjoyed seeing the colour images from an article on K2 in this magazine.

By the end of June we were in position for a summit attempt, marking time in Base Camp waiting for the right weather. The team met in the dining tent after breakfast on June 24 to discuss who should get the first chance to climb to the peak. There was slight tension in the gathering. Personal goals and a realization that this was the summit bid up for grabs created some of the few awkward moments for our team on the entire trip. Each of us had our own reasons to be on the first team. We had all come to Pakistan to climb K2. To follow a dream. But with limited resources established on the mountain, an initial group had to be chosen.

We decided on a three-climber team for the summit bid with a back up team of three others following. The second team would be one day behind on the ridge. Groups of three climbers are a safe number for glacier travel and more capable should something go wrong high on the mountain. Steve was suffering from a virus and had already lost a substantial amount of weight. He looked tired and thin when he told us he wanted to try to help but had justifiable apprehension about his ability to go high. Stacy, the team leader, reserved the right to decide who should be on each team. I did not envy her role.

With exceptional luck, the first team would reach the peak and the following day the second team would have its chance. We knew the odds of getting two groups up a mountain like K2 were very slim. From a practical and historical perspective there seemed little point in even talking about the possibility, as not a single Canadian and only eight Americans had ever reached K2's summit. I wondered if we were somehow raising false hopes for the support team. But to climb only as a support team member with no hope of reaching the top was also too difficult to imagine. Whenever we discussed our plan, we always had the second team attempting the summit.

Stacy listened to the discussion. Everyone felt that Dan and Phil were very healthy, climbing well and eager to go. Logically, they should get the first chance at the summit. Who, then, for the third member? At the time, to create the strongest threesome, Stacy would have been the logical choice. She asked if Dan and I still wanted to reach the top together, a dream we had shared for the past year and a dream of which the entire team was aware. Despite the congestion lingering in my chest, I told Stacy that I would like to try but would approve of any decision she made.

I knew how much she wanted to climb this mountain.

John Haigh had promised his wife that he would only go as high as Camp 4, telling us that reaching 8000 metres was his goal. John Petroske was climbing strongly and methodically, showing his experience from previous trips to the Himalayas. During the team meeting he remained in the background, playing a supporting role in his usual fashion. It was clear that he would play whatever part Stacy thought best for the team. But in his heart John longed to reach the top.

Stacy left the breakfast meeting and went to her tent, alone with her decision, to ponder the alternatives.

At lunch that day, Stacy announced that Phil, Dan and I would form the first summit team and that she, Steve, John Haigh and John Petroske would follow one day behind in support. If Phil, Dan and I got higher than Camp 3 on an attempt without success, the teams would switch roles. If we were foiled by the weather low on the mountain and had to return to Base Camp, the two teams would maintain their position. Everyone thought it was a fair and wise plan. I smiled to myself, happy to be climbing with Dan and Phil in the initial threesome. I hoped for my chest to clear during the present storm period.

The storm lasted another five days.

This graph shows my movement up and down the Abruzzi Ridge in June and July as our team worked hard to establish food and equipment on the mountain. To reach K2's summit, a climber must acclimatize gradually by going high, then returning to lower elevations to rest.

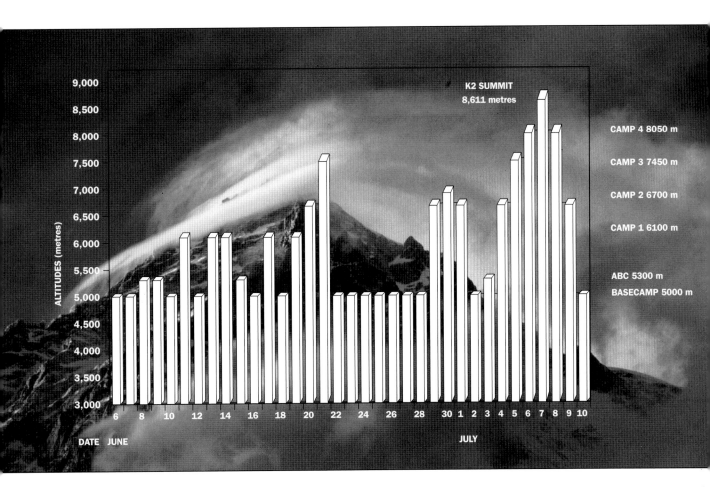

K 2 — D R E A M S A N D R E A L I T Y

Early starts out of Base Camp were normal to ensure we had frozen snow on the Godwin-Austen Glacier. Here Phil and Dan rope up by headlamp before setting out for the glacier on our way to Camp 2 with another load of fuel, food and equipment.

O N JUNE 29 AT 2:00 AM, Dan, Phil and I left for Camp 2 on the chance that the weather might break and allow us to try for the top. The climbing went well considering we had been storm-bound at 5000 metres in Base Camp for seven days. That night, the three of us squeezed inside the tent at 6700 metres but none of us slept very well. Phil was pressed against the upper wall of the tent while Dan fought the feeling of falling off the edge of our platform from his position on the downhill side of our tiny shelter. I was in the middle and felt every movement that either of them made. The rest of our team spent the night in the two tents at Camp 1.

The next morning Phil, Dan and I climbed out of Camp 2, loaded with full packs including our high altitude suits and sleeping gear, expecting to spend that night at Camp 3. Our goal was to push to the summit if the conditions and our bodies permitted. Dan was first on the fixed ropes and carried a heavy load, heavier than Phil or I. He seemed to be acclimatizing well. Phil was next out of Camp 2 and set his usual, steady pace — conserving energy, an important key to his mountaineering success. I was the last to leave. I struggled for over two hours to keep up but could feel the altitude taking control. I was short of breath and stamina, falling further behind my partners with every passing minute. I pondered whether to continue, knowing this could be my only summit chance, but I knew that I had to turn around before becoming a liability for Phil and Dan.

I yelled up that I was returning to Camp 2; I simply did not feel strong enough to go on. They indicated support for my decision but continued upward. Chances to climb a mountain like K2 are few and each opportunity must be seized. Phil passed Dan and broke trail the entire way to Camp 3, tediously lifting the ropes buried under the storm snow with no help from me. I returned by myself to Camp 2.

Sliding down the fixed ropes I knew that I may have missed my chance to achieve my dream, but I was certain that I had made the right decision. Everything had to be perfect to climb to K2's summit; the cost of a mistake was too high. Few people have been above 8000 metres without bottled oxygen. I wondered if I had the mental and physical ability to push myself to the top. As I descended to Camp 2 my brain debated that question intensely.

On reaching Camp 2 I decided to remain there rather than continue down to Base Camp. Acclimatization takes time, I reasoned, different amounts for each person: 6700 metres was an excellent place for my body to adjust to these great heights. To keep myself busy, I began creating another tent platform. Stacy, Steve, John and John were carrying a second tent to Camp 2 and it needed a spot.

Camp 2, like every camp on K2, was terribly exposed. The wind funnels across the South Face of the mountain and rips mercilessly across the Abruzzi Ridge.

                                                                    40

Another hot and sunny red day   June 23
changed to a moisture-laden, eerie evening
of snow falling and a storm system that seems
to be settling in
    I am personally not disappointed to see the
bad weather, my health is not 100% and I
know the opportunity to go up K2 would have
arisen again tomorrow and I would have
had to decline. Selfish reasons but that's
okay because I have no control over the
weather.   Insha alla
    The trip to camp 3 definitely took some steam
out of my sails — my throat is dry and hacky
and the area makes I experienced unsettled
my stomach to the point where eating was
difficult until today. Strength will return
faster now.
    I don't expect to be 100% heading for
the summit, but I'd rather not leave for
basecamp feeling unwell. The mental
drive will have to combine with the
physical body for a reasonable summit
attempt, but there's no point in trying a
mountain like K2 with a strike or two
against.

Motivation and personal health are difficult to maintain over a two or three month expedition; both are crucial ingredients in the complex mix needed to reach the summit of K2.

Tattered remnants of tents from previous expeditions were testimony to the force of the storms which tear at the mountain. I got to work, carving our second tent platform out of the rocks and ice, excavating remains of old equipment, rope and tents frozen in time. The platform was just above our first tent and tucked behind a small rock ridge, partially sheltered from the wind.

Stacy, John Haigh and John Petroske arrived at Camp 2 shortly after 1:00 PM, all feeling strong. Steve had left Camp 1 with them that morning but had gradually fallen behind. My platform was taking shape but still needed plenty of work. Everyone took turns chipping at the rocks and ice which rapidly dulled our climbing axes. After several hours of hard work and difficult breathing at high altitude, sparks and ice chips flying everywhere, we had a second spot. There was room for all of us in two tiny tents. At 4:00 PM we crawled inside and got comfortable, assuming that Steve had returned to Camp 1 and that Phil and Dan were safely in Camp 3.

Torn remains of old tents at the exposed site of Camp 2 at 6700 metres on K2's Abruzzi Ridge.

Whenever the weather turned poor we would retreat from K2 to conserve supplies on the mountain and rest at lower altitude in Base Camp. Steve rappels from House's Chimney on his way down the mountain.

Fixed lines are anchored to the mountain at rock outcrops using pitons. Two or three metal pegs are driven into cracks in the rock like nails creating an anchor, or station, then the ropes are securely fastened to be used for either ascending or descending.

At the scheduled 5:00 PM radio call we heard that Dan and Phil had not been able to find the snowcave at Camp 3. We were surprised when Steve did not come on the air from Camp 1, but decided he was probably working his way down so we would monitor the radio and await his call.

Eight days earlier, Stacy and Doctor John had been the last to Camp 3. They had marked the snowcave with several glacier wands and had left their supplies inside before returning to Base Camp. Now the radio crackled with discussion between Phil in Camp 3 and Stacy in our camp, trying to precisely determine the location of the snow cave in relation to the fixed rope and other features on the mountain. The storm had completely erased all signs of any previous visits.

Dan and Phil needed to find the snowcave. Survival overnight at 7500 metres requires shelter, food and liquid. Inside the buried cave was the fuel, food, equipment and a stove they would need to melt snow for drinks. At 5:30 PM Phil came on the radio and said they had located the top of one wand. They had excavated a large hole in the snow and had located the first shred of evidence of the whereabouts of our cave. After a long day of climbing to Camp 3, both Phil and Dan were tired and at 6:00 PM, with still no sign of the snowcave entrance and the wind shifting to the south, they told us over the radio that they were on their way down. It would be dark in an hour and a half – they made the conservative decision.

Shortly after that call we heard Steve coming up the fixed lines to Camp 2 in a staggering display of persistence. He was in rough shape when he arrived, weak and very tired. Doctor John and I invited him into our tent for soup, drinks and dinner. After an hour of eating and relaxing, Steve crawled out of our crowded two person tent and into the empty Slovenian tent for the night. The following morning he admitted it had been one of the worst times of his life, having to fight for breath through the long night. Doctor John reprimanded him for not informing us of his condition, but Steve had not wanted to disturb our sleep.

At 7:00 PM, Dan and Phil rappelled into Camp 2 for a rest and a drink of water. The five of us at Camp 2 poked our heads out of the tents and congratulated them on their strong efforts at Camp 3. We suggested they stay with us at 6700 metres, but there were no sleeping bags and little room in the tents. Both Dan and Phil felt their best rest would be in Base Camp. Dark was coming quickly. They slipped out of sight down the fixed ropes, reaching Base Camp just after 11:00 PM.

The next morning, July 1, the five of us in Camp 2 woke to blowing snow and a building storm. We descended to Base Camp to wait for better weather – the summit attempt was off.

Time in Base Camp during stormy weather was spent in a variety of personal ways. Typically, Dan would get up at 2:00 AM and walk quickly to the mess tent where he would check the barometer and then look into the night sky for possible clearing or a change of wind direction. I would follow behind, half asleep, shuffling my feet through the snow. John Petroske and John Haigh would listen to the different characteristics in our pace as we passed their tent, wondering what the outcome of that morning's weather forecast would be. Dan's usual comment was that it looked "great" and I would remind him that it was either snowing or the wind remained strong from the south, not the northern wind from China we needed for our summit attempt. Once we had both agreed that the day was not right for climbing on K2, we would go back to sleep until breakfast. Dan was learning patience.

Each morning, anyone who woke up early would head to the kitchen for tea and Ghulam's outlook on things. As to K2, his thoughts were simple, "You climb slowly. If weather is bad, you come here and I cook for you." Sage advice. It was always a very informal assembly. Many mornings our tents would be covered with a fresh coat of snow and the kitchen offered a warm escape from the cold. It was a peaceful time for a cup of chai and some easy discussion.

After breakfast, we tried to ignore the bad weather by holing up in our tents to write letters, to read or to listen to music. Visiting other expeditions on "the Strip" was popular. It was always a treat to try a new type of hot chocolate or some different kind of cookie. The friendly, international flavour at K2 Base Camp made for engaging social visits.

Dinner was the best time for the team to gather and share thoughts. Invariably the discussion would lead to major topics. With our blend of American and Canadian backgrounds, the basis of our taxation systems and the pros and cons of socialized medicine were popular topics. After an hour or so the cold night air would chase us to our tents for some reading by headlamp and the hope that the following day would bring wind from China.

OVERLEAF →
Storms tear at the upper reaches of the mountain most days of the year. The wind from the south is interrupted abruptly by the great height of K2, creating fantastic cloud plumes off the summit.

LEFT
Phil returns to his tent in Base Camp after lunch to read, write letters or listen to some music on one of the many storm days during the summer of 1993 at K2.

Everyone on the team had a high altitude climbing suit, insulated for warmth and fashioned as a one-piece outfit to keep out the wind. Once we climbed above Camp 3 at 7450 metres we wore the suits 24 hours a day.

RIGHT

Dan ascends the cable ladders left behind by previous expeditions on his way to Camp 3 on July 5.

→ OVERLEAF

Dan and Phil plough through the final metres to Camp 3 at 7450 metres through wind compressed snow and sastrugi on July 5.

O N JULY 3 THE entire team left Base Camp at 2:00 AM by headlamp. Phil, Dan and I were hoping to climb to Camp 2, while the others would stay in Camp 1. At the toe of the route in Advanced Base Camp we were chased back down the Godwin-Austen Glacier to Base Camp by worsening weather. A frustrating and tiring false start.

The following morning, Phil, Dan and I tried again and the weather cooperated. Snow conditions were firm underfoot, making for good travel, and we all felt strong climbing on that first day to 6700 metres. The weather was still unsettled but continued to improve, and with the new platform and tent at Camp 2 we slept soundly that night. Stacy, John Haigh and John Petroske moved to Advanced Base Camp for the night, and we spoke with them during the evening radio call. Steve rested in Base Camp.

I lay awake in the early hours of the evening thinking that this might actually be our chance to try for K2's elusive summit. The weather was perfect. The barometer had risen all day and the wind had shifted distinctly to a northerly flow. That thought both excited and scared me. I had no idea what it would be like to climb so high with or without oxygen. I hoped to find out.

The next day dawned clear and the air was still. After a light breakfast of tea and a candy bar, we stuffed our sleeping bags inside our packs, anticipating our first night of the expedition at Camp 3 if we could locate the snowcave. If we failed to find it, we carried enough equipment on our backs to spend the night in a tent. Dan and I wore our high altitude suits to keep our pack weight to a minimum, Phil decided his bulky down suit was too warm to climb in so he chose to carry its weight to our next camp. The fixed ropes showed the way through the now familiar terrain of the Black Pyramid, and the ascent became less of a technical struggle and more of a physical one. In the heat of the day on July 5, the physical demand of the ascent was all I could manage.

I was moving better than I had five days earlier. Perhaps that was due in part to natural acclimatization or perhaps because Doctor John had convinced me to start taking Diamox, a diuretic drug which has had some success, though the findings are inconclusive, in speeding up the process of adapting to altitude.

Phil and Dan took turns ploughing through the final two hundred metres of wind-deposited, storm snow and Dan dropped his pack near the rough location of our Camp 3 at 7450 metres. Exposed to the fury of the prevailing weather from both north and south, Camp 3 is an inhospitable place. As I climbed the last steps toward Phil and Dan, I passed by the site of the Slovenian camp. All that remained was one broken tent pole and a small piece of torn tent material sticking out of the snow. K2 had overwhelmed their camp like the tide engulfing a sandcastle.

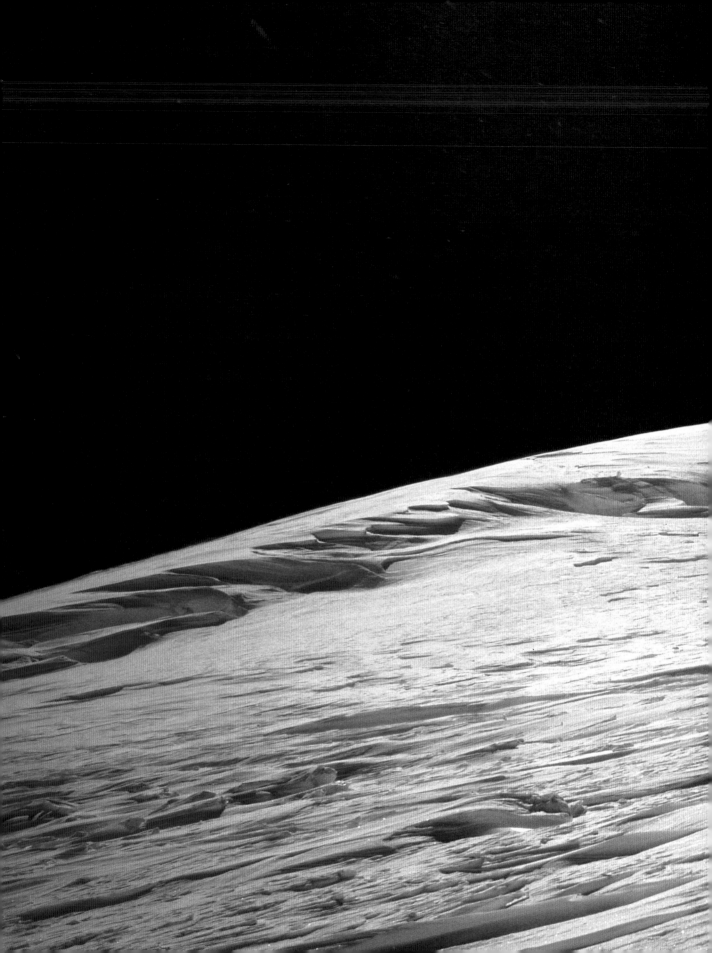

I sat down in the snow and caught my breath. I was hot and felt nauseous but quickly improved with a drink and the removal of some clothing. It was noon and the air was calm and comfortably warm. Dan and Phil unpacked the shovels we had carried from Camp 2 and began the process of excavating the slope in search of our snowcave. I assembled the radio and made the scheduled call to Base Camp. After a full hour of strenuous shovelling Phil struck paydirt. A wand.

It took another hour to dig down through more than a metre of wind-packed storm snow to reclaim our cave. I crawled inside and shovelled for the rest of the afternoon, expanding it until the three of us could lie down comfortably and find shelter. The cool air within the cave was invigorating and allowed me to feel that I was finally doing my share of the work needed to climb K2. We spent the late afternoon and evening brewing up and making dinner in the cave. With my stomach still upset, I skipped dinner and drank only water. I wondered if the Diamox was affecting my appetite or whether it was simply the altitude. But sleep came easily.

The weather on July 6 was perfect. No wind, no clouds, only a sea of peaks in every direction. We roped up for safety against a fall into a crevasse, clipping the 5.5 millimetre Spectra cord to our sit harnesses, and slowly climbed the twenty-five degree glaciated ridge with a plan to establish Camp 4 at over 8000 metres. Even the highest mountains around K2 began to slip below our feet.

Digging the snowcave at Camp 3 was tiring work but provided our team with the comfort and security of shelter in such an exposed place at 7450 metres.

Our team shared a Gamov Bag with the Swedish team at K2 in 1993. The sealed nylon bag is a lightweight pressure chamber that can effectively lower the altitude of any given spot. The air pressure inside the cell is increased with a foot pump and a climber suffering from altitude illness can crawl inside and hope to escape the crippling effects of being too high. In a strong show of endurance, Doctor John carried our Gamov Bag, along with his personal load, all the way to Camp 3 at 7450 metres.

The terrain between Camp 3 and Camp 4 has been the death sentence of many competent climbers caught high on the mountain by changing weather and white-outs. Because of this history, placing glacier wands on the broad ridge has become common practice. On a descent in whiteout conditions the featureless route would be nearly impossible to follow and a weary climber could easily stray off the best line into impassable and dangerous terrain. Our string of green wands with their orange flags, so closely spaced that they resembled a picket fence, looked ridiculous on that brilliant July day, but we wanted to leave as little as possible to chance.

High altitude was beginning to take its toll on us; our pace slowed noticeably. Each step took concentrated effort. Dan and Phil took turns leading our rope, kicking steps in the snow; I was in the middle and placed the wands. The day was hot and we felt the fatigue of both altitude and heat. Every couple of hours we would stop for a drink and to marvel at the scene unfolding below us. I reflected on having not eaten in two days and worried about my energy levels, but the thought of food was repulsive. After seven tiring hours of climbing we had covered scarcely two kilometres of terrain and had gained a mere 600 vertical metres. But Camp 4 was just ahead.

Phil, Dan and I climbed slowly together and stopped as we reached the crest of the ridge at 8000 metres. Dan untied from the rope and continued on toward the uppermost bivouac on our route, Camp 4, still a gruelling day's climb below the summit.

I followed Dan while Phil donned his high altitude suit. The sun was setting behind the bulk of K2 and the temperatures would soon plummet.

Camp 4 was a bleak and windswept place, completely exposed to the awesome power of nature at that height. As I arrived, I dropped my pack and vomited the green bile of an empty stomach. Then I began to shiver. I crawled inside the remains of the Slovenian tent, left behind by that desperate group of men who had struggled for their survival only weeks before.

I felt weak and very small in such a high and wild place.

Phil arrived and together he and Dan erected our small tent. Once our little tent was up, Phil escaped the cold in it while Dan crawled into the Slovenian tent with me and lit the lightweight butane stove. Soon the small gas burner was humming and hot drinks were on the go. Dinner for Dan and Phil meant soup and tea. All I could tolerate was water.

Altitude, combined with anxiousness and cold, produced a fitful sleep for all of us. The alarm rang at midnight. It was time to go.

RIGHT
Dan crests "the Shoulder" at 7900 metres on
K2's Abruzzi Ridge on July 6.

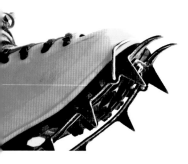

Modern plastic boots with high-tech insulation provide lightweight protection from the cold and excellent performance while climbing. Step-in crampons help to prevent frostbite by eliminating straps which compress the boot and restrict the blood's circulation.

← PREVIOUS LEAF

Sunset on Broad Peak and the four Gasherbrum summits from Camp 4. Clearly illustrating its dominance, K2's shadow is dramatically cast on the horizon to the east in China.

RIGHT

Phil leads toward the Bottleneck with the seracs of K2's summit glacier looming menacingly above. Dan follows methodically in Phil's steps.

AT 2:30 AM I MOVED out of the tent and stepped into my crampons. With clumsy overboots and the first movement of the day at this height, even that simple process was a struggle. My fingers stiffened quickly. It took me fifteen minutes to get organized. Then I left for the top.

The full moon radiated brightly in the cold night sky, casting my shadow to the right, making my headlamp unnecessary. I carried only a water bottle in my pocket and a small camera. Dan followed next, carrying a pack with his big camera and zoom lens, a video camera, water bottle and extra gear inside. The total weight on his back was ten kilograms, a significant amount at 8000 metres. Phil left camp last with a two litre water bag strapped inside his jacket, a small camera, our tiny drug kit of injectable Decadron in case one of us developed high altitude edema and the radio in his pocket.

We were at our physical limits as we climbed above 8000 metres toward the summit of K2. We were not roped together for the summit bid, a decision we all felt was the safest, and the moderate thirty to forty degree snow slopes provided an excellent path to the top. At that altitude it was doubtful any of us could check the fall of a partner without an anchor, and to build anchors in deep snow is a time and energy consuming chore. The conditions we found on K2 were better than we could have hoped for; the snow was soft and secure and the weather perfect. If one of us climbed faster and the others were caught by darkness on the descent, that person could shine a headlamp like a lighthouse to direct the others to Camp 4. For these reasons we decided it would be safest to climb without roping together. Each of us knew we were on our own.

There was a bitter wind blowing down from the summit and my feet and hands were painfully cold. I knew that I should begin to worry about frostbite the minute I lost that sense of pain. We carried no thermometer but the temperature was well below freezing. There was no chance to warm up cold toes and fingers, so I plodded ahead. The altitude kept our pace so slow it was impossible to generate any heat. At that great height, bodies adapt by increasing the red blood cell count. In turn, more oxygen gets to the cellular level, but the blood gets thicker and the risk of cold injury to the toes and fingers increases dramatically. Climbing without the aid of bottled oxygen had been a conscious decision based on style. That decision also increased the risk of our adventure. I was not thinking of biological processes or climbing styles. I was simply cold.

Despite the bitter temperatures it was stunningly beautiful. The icy air had snapped me fully awake and cleared my fuzzy head. A new feeling began to grow inside me: maybe we – I – really would reach the top. Our summit bid was starting out in cold but otherwise perfect weather.

Predictably, just before 6:00 A M, the sun began to make its way over the horizon – hundreds of kilometres away and thousands of metres below us over China. I stared in wonder at the scene below my feet and prayed that the radiant warmth from the sun would quickly thaw my cold extremities and ease my fears of frostbite. I continued to kick steps in the soft snow which was getting steeper as we neared the rocks and slopes above. The effect of the sun's heat slowed the wind descending from the summit and this, more than anything, helped warm our frigid bodies.

I led the way to a small rock ledge and stopped for the first break of the day after more than three hours of climbing. Each of us sipped water from our bottles, put on another layer of sunscreen, lifted our feet off the snow to let the sun warm our boots, and enjoyed the heat. The Bottleneck loomed directly above and appeared to be in good condition.

The Bottleneck is a narrow gully, only a few metres across, of steep, forty-five degree snow and rock, the technical crux of K2's summit day on the Abruzzi Ridge. Some years it is a demanding rock climb; other years it is covered in a thin layer of ice – strenuous and difficult at 8200 metres. Regardless of the conditions, the Bottleneck is always threatened by an intimidating wall of seracs – impending ice towers – which loom menacingly above. During our ascent, the gully was choked with snow from the previous winter, and we made progress in a controlled way, kicking regular steps and trying to conserve energy in the deep snow.

Phil led off from our break with Dan following. The sun continued to rise and our concerns about the cold were replaced an hour later with those of overheating. When I looked ahead at Phil, I could see the butt flap on his puffy down suit was dangling open for ventilation. As for me, I would never have dreamed I would climb towards the summit of the world's second highest peak without a hat on.

As we neared the Bottleneck I was shocked to see Dan slip and fall, sliding by me in the soft snow. But before he had gained any momentum, he was able to stop himself with his ice axe and climb back into our line of steps behind me. It was just a little stumble which thankfully amounted to nothing more than lost effort. The three of us quietly returned to kicking steps in the snow.

Phil climbed through the Bottleneck and waited. I could see him sitting on a rock at the top, watching. I followed his steps across a rocky section to where he was sitting, cautiously placing each crampon on the small holds of rock. I decided that later in the day, on the way down, my route would be a few metres further to the north in the deeper snow of the gully to avoid delicate rock climbing at this great height. Climbing down is always harder than climbing up.

I yelled at Dan to stay in the gully and bypass the rock Phil and I had climbed. Dan was still forty metres behind.

One of the greatest dangers at altitude is dehydration. Water is essential for performance and warding off the symptoms of altitude sickness; a mountaineer climbing should remain as hydrated as possible. On K2, we tried to drink a minimum of 4 litres of water each day.

From the top of the Bottleneck we traversed left above rock cliffs and continued our ascent on snow slopes toward the top, still 350 metres above. Our way to the summit was now only a matter of perseverance and time. We each withdrew into our private mental shells, focused on the task. Our pace was steady but slow; I counted breaths between each step — my mantra — and soon I was up to fifteen deep breaths for every step. I had a new definition of slow, but gradually the terrain fell away below me.

Phil was in front, methodically kicking shin-deep steps in the soft snow, and though I was following his track I could not catch up to him. After we passed the seracs, Phil went up and right in a broad snow corner created by the meeting of the hanging glacier and a snow slope to the left. The snow in the corner was hideous — loose and unconsolidated for over 100 metres, it seemed that every step broke away as it was weighted. Although it was safe, it was a very frustrating and energy consuming section.

While Phil wrestled with the corner, I traversed out to the left and dug a quick test profile in the snow. I was looking for avalanche hazard, knowing the quickest and easiest way down would not be in the corner Phil was presently climbing, but down the slope if it was safe. Deep snow made climbing up that slope impossible, but on descent it would feel very secure. My profile observations confirmed that the snow was stable and I made another decision for the descent.

I rested every once in a while but knew how important it was for us to keep going. Far below, the other members of our team arrived at Camp 4. Stacy, John Haigh and John Petroske looked like ants on a sidewalk from our vantage point just below the summit.

The views were spectacular. Mountains in all directions. These were the peaks I grew up reading about: Broad Peak and the four Gasherbrum summits to the east, the Latok peaks, the Ogre and Mustagh Tower to the southwest and Masherbrum and Chogolisa to the southeast. They all became part of me; no longer pictures in a book or words on a page, they would be real peaks in my memory. And K2. Now I could say I knew K2. I had climbed on its rock, slept on its flanks and huddled from the wind behind its ridges. And incredibly, we were near its summit.

On July 7, 1993 at 2:57 PM, twelve hours after leaving Camp 4, Phil became the ninth American to reach the top of K2 at 8611 metres. He looked out at Gasherbrum II, an 8000 metre peak he had climbed in 1987 ,and later said, "It looked tiny." I could see him near the top, less than 200 metres from me but still a formidable distance away at my present pace. Phil radioed Base Camp from the peak to find that the entire Strip was tuned in. Barry Blanchard, who was at K2 with fellow Canadians Peter Arbic and Troy Kirwan attempting a bold, alpine style ascent of the South Pillar,

RIGHT

Phil leads the traverse above the Bottleneck, working very hard in deep snow. From the end of the traverse he led for the rest of the day, all the way to the summit.

Communication is important in most things in life and climbing mountains is no exception. To stay in touch with Base Camp regarding team movement, planning logistics or weather conditions we used small, portable radios while climbing on the upper reaches of K2.

RIGHT

I sat down just below the summit to wait for Dan and stared with wonder at the scene below my feet. The Godwin-Austen Glacier flows to Concordia where it meets the Baltoro Glacier. The tiny white dome on the horizon is the fabled summit of Chogolisa – 7655 metres.

jested Phil, "I can't believe there's a hick from Wyoming on the summit of K2." In a tone mixed with pride and excitement Yousaf said, "Phil, I am taking your picture while you are on top of K2. You will not be able to see you in this picture but you will know you are there because I am taking it now, while you are on top of K2." Stacy came on the radio from Camp 4 and asked, "Phil, where are you?" Phil responded, "I'm on the tippy top!" He snapped a picture of himself and then turned around and began the descent.

Phil and I met on his way down. We hugged and spoke briefly together. Always concerned about safety, Phil asked if I would consider turning around due to the late hour of the day. His worry was that I was still some distance from the top and the descent would be challenging or impossible in the dark. I told him that I was feeling in control and would continue with my climb. I thought the descent would go quickly.

We talked about Dan and his progress. We were both troubled that Dan, who had kept up a good pace the entire climb to Camp 4, was now falling behind. Phil said he would speak with Dan and suggest he turn around and descend with him. He then asked if I wanted the radio and the high altitude drugs he carried in his pocket. I declined that offer. I stood and watched Phil cautiously pick his way down the route toward Dan, several hundred metres away. I noticed that Dan had left his pack far below, finally dropping the weight which was slowing him down; even a few kilograms at that height can make a difference. They embraced. The Swedish team in Base Camp watched that show of emotion through their powerful telescope. Phil asked Dan to descend with him but Dan said, "I gotta go." Phil continued on his way down to Camp 4, descending out of sight, leaving the radio and the drug kit in Dan's pack. Dan and I exchanged a wave of acknowledgement, then we both returned to the task at hand – the final metres to the top.

Fifty minutes after Phil, I reached a point only five metres below K2's grand summit and stopped to wait for Dan. We had decided long ago to try to make the first Canadian ascent of the mountain together. So I carved a platform and sat down in the afternoon sun. A more magical experience would be hard to imagine.

I stared out at the countless mountains below me and simply absorbed the wonder of it all. In every direction lay peaks and glaciers: some world famous, many unnamed, all part of a remarkable creation. It was a wondrous time for me, alone in that place, only faintly aware that I was sitting at 8600 metres on one of the world's most challenging and treacherous mountains. It was 3:50 PM, and time seemed to stand still.

Forty-five minutes later, Dan climbed into view. Together we took the final steps to the top. It was one of my life's extraordinary moments.

I snapped two photographs of Dan to capture the instant. We had shared a dream and realized it in almost storybook fashion. I thought of my family and friends, people who had supported me through the years, allowing me to reach such a place. Years of climbing and mountain experience had led to that moment. Dan and I hugged on K2's peak. My breathing got even more difficult as an emotional lump formed in my throat.

With the ascent of K2, Dan, a man who had taken to mountaineering only seven years before, joined a rare band of adventurous climbers who had reached the summit of both K2 and Mount Everest — a feat accomplished by fewer people on Earth than have flown in space.

On the top Dan took off his mitts and with cold fingers fumbled with the two cameras he had carried up inside his suit. First he shot some video then some stills. He took photographs with us holding the Canadian flag, then environmental banners designed to raise the profile of two wilderness land-use issues we were concerned about back home in British Columbia: clear-cut logging in Clayoquot Sound and a huge strip mine near the Tatshenshini River. Neither of us could have known that the Tatshenshini River had been preserved in its entirety only two weeks before, yet both of us knew how exploring British Columbia's wilderness helped shape our lives.

Time drifted past. My hands got cold. By 4:55 PM it was time to leave the top. The wind had shifted and the weather was changing. Our luck had run out. Very suddenly the afternoon air began to lose its heat and the pleasant pinnacle of K2 became a place of potential danger. I had stuck around on the summit for over an hour and knew it was time to go. We turned our backs to K2's peak and carefully began the process of descending to Camp 4.

Each step down the mountain required concentration. I was very aware of the risk of stumbling or catching a crampon, careful of every foot placement and consciously assessing the quality of the snow to make sure there were no surprises. The upper mountain consisted of hard-packed snow, compressed by the wind which pours across K2's ridges and faces. After half an hour of carefully choosing our way, we gratefully stepped into the deep snow of the sheltered slope where I had earlier dug my observation pit. Here we relaxed somewhat and plunged down in the soft snow for twenty minutes. Everything was going well; we were tired but descending steadily.

It was 6:15 PM by the time I traversed to the Bottleneck, only 300 metres above Camp 4. Dan was several minutes behind and I decided this was convenient as we could downclimb the Bottleneck separately. I continued facing out and very carefully began the descent of the gully. Occasionally, as the soft snow gave way and my

← PREVIOUS LEAF

At 4:35 PM on July 7, 1993, Dan Culver and I became the first Canadians to reach the summit of K2, the world's second highest mountain. The sea of peaks to the north in China provided an inspiring background for the summit photo of Dan.

K2 — DREAMS AND REALITY

98

crampons scraped on the rocks below, I instinctively fought to keep my balance. Fatigue and terrain combined and I had a few awkward stumbles in the Bottleneck, but slowly the worst of it was behind me.

Camp 4 was just below and, as in the morning, my crampons dug confidently into the hard surface. I began the traverse towards Camp 4 and glanced up to see that Dan was entering the Bottleneck. Summit day was almost over. Finally. I wanted to relax and enjoy our success.

Seconds later my brain was brutally invaded by a loud, crashing noise, a noise which in an instant shattered the silence and the harmony of the day. I spun around to see Dan cartwheeling violently through the snow, rolling by me at high speed. I stared in horror. All I could see was Dan tumbling faster and faster, his blonde hair in the tangle of the fall. As he hit the hard snow below me his limp body began gaining momentum. Only a miracle would stop him.

There was no miracle.

I watched Dan hit some small rocks 100 metres below then continue to fall down a broad chute gaining speed with every passing second. He disappeared from my sight. I wanted not to believe.

My throat seized up in a swell of emotion. Weakly I croaked for help. Camp 4 was only 200 metres away. I yelled for help again, hoping that someone would hear. Then I cried out for Dan and listened. Nothing. I followed the line of his fall and carefully picked my way down through the rocks. The marks in the hard snow became farther and farther apart, spans of more than thirty metres, as his body had bounded down the face.

Gravity.

I found his hat.

My legs were tired and the steepening terrain of the South Face was the last place I wanted to be. I stopped on a ledge and stared down the huge expanse of the mountain at my feet. There was no sign of Dan. Nothing. I yelled his name for what seemed the hundredth time. There was no response. I sat down on the ledge in disbelief.

Dan was dead.

The salty taste of the tears rolling off my cheeks into my cracked lips brought me slowly back to the world of reality. I knew in my head that Dan was gone, yet my heart was yearning to refuse that logic. I was alone, sitting on a ledge just below 8000 metres and looking down the immense South Face of K2, wondering where Dan's body would come to rest. I took no solace then, in the thin cold air, knowing that Dan's spirit would remain with many of us forever. Thoughts like that were for another time. For me it was time to brave the descent of K2 without him.

Through the haze of emotion and altitude I assessed my situation. First, I had to climb back up to Camp 4, and painstakingly regain the several hundred metres of terrain which I had lost trying to find Dan. Time was still moving relentlessly ahead and glancing at my watch I realized we — rather, I — had been climbing for over fifteen hours above 8000 metres. I was physically exhausted and had just ridden an emotional roller coaster to the bottom of the big hill. It had been three days since my last morsel of food. Darkness would eclipse the Karakoram mountains in less than an hour. I had to shift into a pattern of decisions which would allow me to survive. I remembered vaguely that the wind had shifted too — a storm was coming.

It was time to be careful, not a time for mistakes. I felt weak and sad but determined to make it safely back to Camp 4. It took half an hour for me to manage the terrain back to the ridge. As I climbed slowly over the crest of the ridge I met Stacy, John and John. They were all geared up with ropes, first aid equipment and the energy to help with a rescue. There was nothing they could do. I told them through tears that Dan had died; then I fell backwards in the snow. John and John helped me to my feet and we all shared an embrace. The first of many. I remember walking carelessly across the flat ridge to the tent.

Phil was making hot drinks as I crawled into our tent. I tried to reflect on what had just happened. In the background, I could hear Stacy talking to Yousaf in Base Camp, relating the news of Dan's fall. Yousaf would take it hard; he and Dan had become good friends.

Dan. I wondered if he was out there somewhere? I fought to get my boots off in the cold. Insulated overboots always make it tougher to reach the laces. Maybe he was badly hurt. I pulled my down sleeping bag around my shoulders and slumped to the back of the tent. Was he bleeding? Barely clinging to a rock? Phil passed me a cup of warm water and I sipped it appreciatively. If anyone could survive such a huge fall it would be Dan. God knows there had been other close calls. I felt very tired. Could he still be alive? My imagination tried to dominate my logical brain.

I knew Dan was dead.

Very quickly it turned to night and the wind was building from the south. I knew he was dead.

The hot water tasted good. My cool fingers wrapped around the warm mug and gratefully absorbed the heat. I still could not imagine the thought of anything but water. No food. The night air was getting colder by the minute but my sleeping bag was warm. After one more drink I was finished for the day. I needed some sleep.

THE STORM CAME to full force around 3:00 AM. I guess we knew it would; the wind shift and the plummeting barometer had warned us. I coughed through the night keeping both myself and Phil awake. Phil was anxiously listening to the cough, hoping I did not develop any fluid. It remained a dry, irritating hack which was good; no high altitude edema in my lungs. Phil leaned against the tent wall to reduce the stress from the powerful wind on the poles and waited for daylight. There were five of us camped at just over 8000 metres: Phil, Stacy, John Haigh, John Petroske and myself. At first light, Stacy looked outside her tent and announced that the visibility was only ten metres. Gusts of wind lashed at our small tents, threatening to tear them from the mountain. My thoughts went out to Dan, wishing him well, knowing I would never see him again.

By 8:00 AM we had packed up our tents and equipment and left Camp 4. We stumbled from wand to wand towards Camp 3 in fierce winds and near-zero visibility. The fifteen metre spacing of our glacier wands now seemed barely enough. Phil led the way, assessing our route for any new avalanche hazard from wind-loaded snow. Ice crystals driven by the wind stung my face. The noise was constant and intense. There was no relief from this unrelenting attack on my senses. Just surviving helped me to forget.

We dragged ourselves into the snowcave at Camp 3, grateful for a quiet break from the ruthless, hurricane-force winds outside. The silence and comfort of the cave was a remarkable contrast to the pounding of the mountain's storm only two metres away. I ripped the goggles off my face and peeled two centimetres of wind-driven ice from around the edges.

Soon there was warm water on the stove and the comfort of a small hole in the snow with five friends crammed inside. The respite from the storm allowed thoughts of Dan to once again surface in my brain. It was going to be a difficult time. I leaned back, closed my eyes and saw Dan. I could not get him off my mind. Again I wondered if he had survived the fall and was hurt but still alive on the South Face somewhere. These thoughts were illogical. I had seen his fall. I had watched him die. Still my mind invented several images. I hated this picture of Dan: bloody, alone and waiting to die, the storm raging around him. With great effort, I drove those visions from my head.

Dan was gone.

After a brief two-hour break at Camp 3 we slid out the cave's entrance to face the elements once more. Instantly, we were back into survival mode. The wind slapped my face without mercy. Exhausted, I turned my back and prepared to descend. Phil had left his pack outside the snowcave's entrance and it was gone; blown off the mountain. His camera, clothing, sleepingbag – everything. Gone. We had to get off K2 to escape the storm and the deadly effects of high altitude.

From the snowcave entrance we had fixed ropes as a guide, but the weather continued to batter us as we rappelled through the Black Pyramid, dangling on the lines. The wind manhandled me again and again, throwing me into the rocks. John Haigh was lifted by gusts and slammed into the mountain. What had taken only an hour in calm weather turned into three hours of stress and survival in the intensity of the storm. Without the preparation and effort of the past month, our descent would have been impossible. At least the way was familiar and manageable; we just needed to be careful.

I reached Camp 2 at 2:30 PM and had already decided to stay the night. I was too weak to continue and was worried that I could make a mistake if I pushed on. Phil, Stacy and John Haigh left for Base Camp, arriving there just after dark. Peter Arbic and Ghulam hiked out to meet them and while Peter coiled the rope Ghulam hugged his friends and said only, "Sorry." Late that night, Phil sat in Ghulam's tent drinking tea. Ghulam said, "Now, you promise, never return to K2." Phil promised. John Petroske had volunteered to stay in Camp 2 with me. Together we waited out the night at 6700 metres.

The storm continued into the night's darkness. John and I curled deeper into our sleeping bags and hoped it would go away. Both of us were happy that our team had made the effort and that our tent was sheltered behind the small rock ridge at Camp 2. The other tents — the Swedish and Dutch — were being pummelled harshly by the weather and were on the verge of being destroyed. John and I were alone on K2.

We woke at first light on July 9 to find the storm raging unabated. After a brief radio contact with Base Camp, relieved to hear that Stacy, John Haigh and Phil had reached there safely the night before, we crawled out of our tent and faced the powerful winds and driving snow. We had rested for sixteen hours which helped us to concentrate despite the noise and fury of the wind. We set up each rappel with care. Neither of us wanted a mistake.

Two hours later, just after 10:00 AM, we rappelled into Camp 1 and dove into the small tent, still wearing all of our equipment. Neither of us worried about the impact of a careless crampon on the delicate nylon walls. Escape was all we craved. We would come back later to clean our gear from the mountain.

After thirty minutes inside our shelter at Camp 1, we stepped back into the storm and continued down the ropes leading to Advanced Base Camp. It took two hours to reach the bottom of the Abruzzi and I felt very weak. It had been more than four days since I had eaten anything and my energy had been sapped by the days above 7500 metres combined with the emotional drain of Dan's death. The weight of my pack was too much and I abandoned it right there. I would come back and get it another time.

From Advanced Base Camp I gratefully followed John's lead across the Godwin-Austen Glacier towards Base Camp. Finally, we were off the mountain.

The walk was frustrating. We were tired and impatient to be in Base Camp as soon as possible, but the warming snowpack on the glacier would barely support our weight. Every few steps one of our legs would poke through the surface crust. I felt like screaming. The struggle to recover from knee-deep holes was sucking the last reserves of my strength. I was letting go. Sensing that we were off the mountain and past any real hazard, I let my guard drop and nearly abandoned my physical will to continue. We had crossed this familiar terrain more than fifteen times during June and early July while preparing for our final ascent of the mountain, but this trip across the Godwin-Austen Glacier was the slowest and most difficult.

Then we heard a loud crack high up in the clouds on K2.

I saw John look up. Wearily I followed his gaze and saw nothing, only the thick, low ceiling of clouds shrouding the surrounding mountain walls, completely blocking our view of the upper slopes of K2 and Broad Peak. We shrugged our shoulders and turned our energy back to the disheartening snow.

Two steps later the loud rumble turned into a huge avalanche pouring out of the clouds. The South Face of K2 had released its storm snow.

Run!

Where? There was nowhere to go. After an instant of panic, John and I turned our backs to the onrushing snow and dropped to our knees. At least there was a kilometre of flat glacier between us and the base of K2's South Face to take some of the energy out of the avalanche.

It hit with such force John was immediately blown from my side. I felt the air being sucked out of me. I could not breathe. I was being pushed along the flat glacier on my hands and knees by the force of the blast. The wind was overwhelming. It was as though I was caught in a turbulent riptide, completely helpless in the power of the avalanche's wave. I prayed that the sweep of snow contained only powder, no chunks of serac ice or large rocks. Their impact would surely be crippling. Or deadly.

The powerful initial blast must have lasted only a few seconds but it seemed like several long minutes. Then the speed of the avalanche gradually slowed and snow began building up around me. Fortunately, when its energy was spent the deposit was only twenty centimetres of loose snow. I marvelled at the might and the mercy of nature's forces.

I looked around and saw John, five metres away, wrapped in the rope like a

Christmas present. He stood up and dusted himself off. We smiled weakly at each other and I said, "John, let's just go home."

We stumbled across the flat glacier toward the moraine where our Base Camp was located. In the distance, I saw four people coming to greet us. As we neared I could see it was Phil and my three Canadian friends: Troy, Peter and Barry. They had come to accompany John and me on our last steps into Base Camp.

The meeting was filled with emotion. I felt secure in their arms but the affection and friendship of their long embraces again brought my feelings of sorrow and loss to the surface from my purposely hidden reservoirs deep inside. I let go, too tired to care about anything else. Tears poured out.

The final few hundred metres among the scattered rocks to our Base Camp were unusually quiet. Thankfully. Snow was falling lightly and the Dutch, Catalonian and British teams were resting inside their tents as we crept silently through their camps. My spirit was at rock bottom. I had no energy to tell our story. Had I been less tired and thinking more clearly I would have known that it did not matter — each climber, no matter the country, knew the makings of our tale. Though it was personal for me, for K2 it was generic. K2 kills climbers.

Everyone kept tent doors closed and left our account for another time. They knew that in a few days or weeks — during the next clear weather from the north in China — they might be feeling as I was, living their own tragic saga after a summit bid on the mountain.

Walking into Base Camp stirred yet more emotion. Reunited with my friends, Dan's friends, made me feel like I was the luckiest person alive. All of us wept.

Death is trying for those who are left behind. To attempt to express our deep feelings and pain is something few people have much practice at. Probably a good thing. All of us stopped trying to talk about what had happened and instead escaped the foul weather inside our dining tent. I sat in a back corner and listened to the others while I sipped at a bowl of hot broth from Ghulam's kitchen. It had been five days since my last scrap of food. My stomach was still queasy but the soup was delicious.

Eventually, after a second warm drink and some moments of uneasy conversation, I excused myself and went to the tent Dan and I had shared in Base Camp. I wanted to get out of my harness, boots and suit; I reeked of days-old urine. Now that I was off the mountain I could not stand my own stench. The inner layers of my clothing were stuck to my body. I wanted to get out of everything associated with K2.

The tent was just as we had left it, although the platform of rock and ice it rested on had melted slightly after six days. As a passing thought, I realized I would

RIGHT

The dying light of the day in K2 Base Camp created spectacular colour on Chogolisa.

→ OVERLEAF

Porters returning home after carrying loads to Gasherbrum II for a Swiss expedition.

have to move our tent again soon. Inside, everything of Dan's was still there. All his books, his journal, letters from home to be opened after the summit, good luck charms sent by friends hanging from the roof, pictures taped to the tent wall — everything. My emotional purging was going to take a long time.

I peeled off my suit and long underwear. I stripped down to nothing and threw all the disgusting inner layers out the door into the snow. I smelled terrible.

My skin tingled in the cool air.

I stared in disbelief at my naked body. I had withered away to nothing. My muscles had shrivelled and gone; my legs felt soft and flabby. I saw only skin and bones. K2 had taken its physical toll of me. Changing into clean cotton, I crawled inside my sleeping bag and slept deeply for the rest of the afternoon.

K2 — DREAMS AND REALITY

CLIMBING A MOUNTAIN LIKE K2 needs to be done for the right reasons. There is great risk. No one can deny that. If there was no risk, if the summit was easily attained, if the climb was a certain bet, then K2 would be of little interest to mountaineers. The unknown is important. Exploring new places and attempting to personally meet the test of the mountain is a critical part of the experience.

We went to K2 seeking adventure.

Our team's stated purpose was to reach the summit of K2 and descend in as safe a manner as possible, to build and strengthen friendships with team members and to remove all traces of our presence once we were done. It was an admirable goal and even including the tragedy of Dan's fall our team feels we accomplished our objectives.

Mistakes happen. Errors in judgement. The line between living and dying above 8000 metres is very fine. It may have been that both Phil and I were close to crossing that line. There are so few places like the top of K2 on Earth that it is nearly impossible to prepare for such a journey. When we make the decision to go to that kind of a mountain – a mountain like K2 – we rely heavily on experience and instinct. We count on years of climbing other mountains and long hours spent on snow, ice and rock in every condition. Those are the only sources we have to draw on when a difficult moment arises.

Dan's ice axe was found in the Bottleneck three weeks after his fall by a Danish climber, Raphael Jensen, on his way to the top of K2. Perhaps Dan blacked out and left it there. It is possible he was hit on the head with a chunk of ice and dropped his axe. No one will ever know exactly what happened. Twenty years ago I was told by my first mountaineering instructor that "An ice axe is the mountaineer's tool. Learn how to use your axe, be comfortable with it in both hands and never let go." Maybe Dan's climbing career took him to a place like the Bottleneck too soon. Maybe not.

I would never have reached K2's summit had it not been for Dan. I learned from him what it took to climb such a mountain. How to focus on the task and maintain motivation after weeks of waiting. How to achieve your dream when others are willing to let it go. His positive outlook and energy helped carry me to the top.

Where does ambition fit into the decision-making process? This was a question I continually asked myself, and honesty is important because the stakes are very high.

Five climbers died on the mountain during the summer of 1993. A young Swede, Daniel Bidner, who had become our friend, collapsed in the snow at 8300

RIGHT

This memorial cairn was erected by American climbers in 1953 after one of their teammates – Art Gilkey – vanished mysteriously in an avalanche at 7100 metres on the Abruzzi Ridge. Since then, dozens of the world's best mountaineers have been enshrined at the Gilkey Memorial after losing their lives on K2.

metres after reaching K2's summit — he died of altitude and exhaustion. Two Germans, Peter Mezger and Reamer Joswig — both fifty years old — fell while descending from the top on July 30, the same day as Bidner. Bostjan Kekec, the twenty-three-year-old Slovenian, died of cerebral edema at 8000 metres. And Dan. Historically, the total of fatalities on K2 stands at thirty-three. Only ninety-three have ever reached the top. Whether all of those who died understood the risk of their ascent and the consequences of their death, I do not know. I do know the impact of Dan's loss has been profound on me and his many loved ones.

Our success on K2 was something to celebrate. Our team came back to North America as close friends. After safety, that is the most important consideration. We managed, with the help of other teams, to clean K2 of everything but our fixed ropes. When we left Base Camp, those lines were still being used by five other expeditions on the Abruzzi Ridge. We carried everything of ours and hundreds of kilograms of others' garbage out from the mountains. The environment needs everyone's help.

Down the list, but still important to all of us, was the accomplishment we achieved on the mountain. Phil became the ninth American, and Dan and I the first Canadians to ascend this great peak — the world's second highest mountain and one of mountaineering's ultimate challenges. For Phil and for me it will always be an extraordinary moment. A moment we can call on at any time. To cherish. To help us smile when times are hard. It is our moment.

But it was exactly that — a moment. To have the choice of giving up that moment and having Dan back would be an easy decision.

Unfortunately, that is a decision none of us can make.

RIGHT

A letter from my brother that I received by mail runner on July 22 at Korophon Tsok on our trek out of the mountains. His words stirred my temporarily dormant emotions and left me craving home.

→ OVERLEAF

Sunset in the Karakoram

attention, and no sign of slowing down.

Anyhow, Jim m'bro, I imagine this experience will overshadow some of the other lifeshaker/personmakers, like the Bunsby fall and the MacArthur gurgle. Remember you are still Jim the mountain guide, getting stronger everyday and learning from everything around you. That's what has kept you alive through too many close ones, don't blow it now... I need you here. Dan is dead, but all of us have to carry a piece of him with us — and for all of ♯ us, that will be a real good piece to add on. Dan had a special something.

Matt (I called him) had an interesting perspective. He commented on how each of us as individuals accept risk in our lives for ourselves, and feel it is our right to make these decisions. Yet we don't carry all of the risk — no doubt Patti feels that she bore and is bearing a huge part of Dan's risk decision. All of us feel a loss to have him gone. Hopefully all of us learn from this decision Dan made and carry on.

I miss you, Jim, and after this accident feel that I want to see you just to make sure you're still there. Kind of wierd, but maybe my (and others') imagination has got you into trouble since Monday when we heard, and even though we know that you're OK the flesh is the truth of the pudding. If you decide to hang out in Pakistan or travel the Silk Road, be sure to let us know! There've been lots of people asking me when you get home, I keep saying end of the month or early August. I expect that you'll live up to the earlier commitment to a clean trip, this early finish must mean more gear and more porters on the way out. Hope it doesn't break you any worse.

Car is running great, thanks again. I use the Honda mostly, but am comforted to know that there is a car here for Vick and Jas if they need one.

C.U. soon, Jim, and take care on the trip home. Lots of Love,

Kev

K2
DREAMS AND REALITY